Quick Tips
Paper Crafts

by Rebecca Ludens and Jennifer Schmidt

Wiley Publishing, Inc.

Paper Crafts VISUAL™ Quick Tips

Copyright © 2008 by Wiley Publishing, Inc., Hoboken, New Jersey. All rights reserved.

Published by Wiley Publishing, Inc., Hoboken, New Jersey

No part of this publication may be reproduced, stored in a retrieval system or transmitted in any form or by any means, electronic, mechanical, photocopying, recording, scanning or otherwise, except as permitted under Sections 107 or 108 of the 1976 United States Copyright Act, without either the prior written permission of the Publisher, or authorization through payment of the appropriate per-copy fee to the Copyright Clearance Center, 222 Rosewood Drive, Danvers, MA 01923, (978) 750-8400, fax (978) 646-8600, or on the web at www.copyright.com. Requests to the Publisher for permission should be addressed to the Legal Department, Wiley Publishing, Inc., 10475 Crosspoint Blvd., Indianapolis, IN 46256, (317) 572-3447, fax (317) 572-4355, or online at http://www.wiley.com/go/permissions.

Wiley, the Wiley Publishing logo, Teach Yourself VISUALLY, and related trademarks are trademarks or registered trademarks of John Wiley & Sons, Inc. and/or its affiliates. All other trademarks are the property of their respective owners. Wiley Publishing, Inc. is not associated with any product or vendor mentioned in this book.

The publisher and the author make no representations or warranties with respect to the accuracy or completeness of the contents of this work and specifically disclaim all warranties, including without limitation warranties of fitness for a particular purpose. No warranty may be created or extended by sales or promotional materials. The advice and strategies contained herein may not be suitable for every situation. This work is sold with the understanding that the publisher is not engaged in rendering legal, accounting, or other professional services. If professional assistance is required, the services of a competent professional person should be sought. Neither the publisher nor the author shall be liable for damages arising here from. The fact that an organization or Website is referred to in this work as a citation and/or a potential source of further information does not mean that the author or the publisher endorses the information the organization or Website may provide or recommendations it may make. Further, readers should be aware that Internet Websites listed in this work may have changed or disappeared between when this work was written and when it is read.

For general information on our other products and services or to obtain technical support please contact our Customer Care Department within the U.S. at (800) 762-2974, outside the U.S. at (317) 572-3993 or fax (317) 572-4002.

Wiley also publishes its books in a variety of electronic formats. Some content that appears in print may not be available in electronic books. For more information about Wiley products, please visit our web site at www.wiley.com.

Library of Congress Control Number: **2008924511**

ISBN: 978-0-470-22852-4

Printed in China

10 9 8 7 6 5 4 3 2 1

Book production by Wiley Publishing, Inc. Composition Services

Wiley Bicentennial Logo: Richard J. Pacifico

Praise for the VISUAL Series

I just had to let you and your company know how great I think your books are. I just purchased my third Visual book (my first two are dog-eared now!) and, once again, your product has surpassed my expectations. The expertise, thought, and effort that go into each book are obvious, and I sincerely appreciate your efforts. Keep up the wonderful work!

—Tracey Moore (Memphis, TN)

I have several books from the Visual series and have always found them to be valuable resources.

—Stephen P. Miller (Ballston Spa, NY)

Thank you for the wonderful books you produce. It wasn't until I was an adult that I discovered how I learn—visually. Although a few publishers out there claim to present the material visually, nothing compares to Visual books. I love the simple layout. Everything is easy to follow. And I understand the material! You really know the way I think and learn. Thanks so much!

—Stacey Han (Avondale, AZ)

Like a lot of other people, I understand things best when I see them visually. Your books really make learning easy and life more fun.

—John T. Frey (Cadillac, MI)

I am an avid fan of your Visual books. If I need to learn anything, I just buy one of your books and learn the topic in no time. Wonders! I have even trained my friends to give me Visual books as gifts.

—Illona Bergstrom (Aventura, FL)

I write to extend my thanks and appreciation for your books. They are clear, easy to follow, and straight to the point. Keep up the good work! I bought several of your books and they are just right! No regrets! I will always buy your books because they are the best.

—Seward Kollie (Dakar, Senegal)

Credits

Acquisitions Editor
Pam Mourouzis

Project Editor
Donna Wright

Copy Editor
Marylouise Wiack

Editorial Manager
Christina Stambaugh

Publisher
Cindy Kitchel

Vice President and Executive Publisher
Kathy Nebenhaus

Interior Design
Kathie Rickard
Elizabeth Brooks

Cover Design
José Almaguer

Photography
Matt Bowen

About the Authors

Rebecca Ludens (Kalamazoo, MI) is the Scrapbooking Guide for About.com, where she writes weekly articles, product reviews, and how-tos. She has created scrapbook page designs for several scrapbooking manufacturers and has appeared on the television show DIY Scrapbooking and at scrapbook shows, retreats, and cruises.

Jennifer Schmidt (Crystal Lake, IL) has been on the design team for several scrapbooking manufacturers. She has been teaching scrapbooking classes for over eight years at conventions across the country, and has had pages published in scrapbooking magazines as well as having pages displayed on DIY Scrapbooking.

Acknowledgments

Thank you to all the photographers, both professional and amateur, who allowed us to use their photos on scrapbook pages in this book: Shea Wetzler of Shea Photography, Linda Curtin, Carolyn Meyers, Dara Ludens, Julie Gehring, Heidi Lachel, and Barb Obley.

Thank you, also, to our husbands (Douglas Ludens and Brian Schmidt) who were so patient and supportive during the process of writing this book. And, of course, thank you to our children (all eight of them between the two of us) who are our constant scrapbooking inspiration—Bethany, Lindsey, and Mikhail Ludens; Elizabeth, Kaitlyn, Rachel, Steven, and Philip Schmidt.

Table of Contents

Introduction to Paper Crafts

Types of Paper. 4
Cut It Up 5
Choose Adhesives. 6
Other Supplies 8
Use a Color Wheel 10
Color Scheme Examples. 12
Create a Mood with Color 14

Getting Started Scrapbooking

Why Scrapbook?. 18
Choose Your Album 20
Common Album Sizes 21
The Basics of a Layout 22
Make Your First Page 23
Mat a Photo. 24
Matting Techniques. 25
Create a Focal Point 26
Scrapbook Page Gallery. 28

Card Making Basics

Envelope Sizes 34
Scoring and Folding 35
Make Your Own Envelopes 36
Photo Greeting Cards. 38
Match Book Invitations. 40
File Folder Cards. 42
Make a Library Pocket Card. 44
Window Cards 46
Pop-Up Cards 49
Dry Embossing Cards and Envelopes 52
Birthday Card Organizer 54
Recipe Book 57
Card Gallery 58

Book Making

Basic Mini-Book 64
Baby's First Year Mini-Book 68
Mini-Book on a Scrapbook Page 69
Envelope Book 70
Travel-Themed Envelope Book 73
Accordion Book 74
Paper Bag Book 78
Friends Paper Bag Book 81
Container Books 82

Stamping

Types of Stamps 88
Ink Pads and Cleaners 90
Stamping Lettering 92
Stamping with Bleach 94
Pieced Stamping 96
Double Stamping 98
Heat Embossing 100
Embellishing Stamping 102

Crafting Techniques

Texture on Paper.................................. 108
Inking... 110
Chalking... 111
Geometric Borders 112
Serendipity Squares 114
Paper Piecing.................................... 116
Sewing on Paper.................................. 120
Folded Paper Ribbon 122
Vellum Envelope 124
Quilling 126
Quilling Combined Shapes......................... 129
Quilling a Bouquet of Roses...................... 130
Eyelets 132
Brads 134
Silk Flowers 136

Lettering Styles

Printing on Vellum 140

Printing on Transparencies........................... 142

Printing on Cork, Fabric, and Ribbon 144

Printing on Tags and Die-Cuts 146

Label Maker Lettering............................... 148

Stamping and Templates 150

Layered Letters 152

Shaker Letters 154

Tag Shaker Titles 156

Chipboard Monogram Letters 158

Clay Letters 162

Stencil Paste Letters 164

Adding Artistic Flair

Collage Wall Art 168

Tissue Paper Decoupage 170

Art Journaling 172

Sample Art Journals 174

Artist Trading Cards................................. 176

Artist Trading Card Gallery 178

Crafting Home Décor

Wooden Photo Cubes.................................. 182
Photo Cube Puzzle 184
Decorated Photo Frames 186
Paper Pieced and Decoupaged Lamp 188
Scrapbooking on Canvas 190
Sparkle Lights 192
Tween Mobile 194
Art Clock 196
Letter Blocks 198

Appendix: Patterns 200
Index 210

chapter 1

Introduction to Paper Crafts

Paper crafting is anything that uses paper to express your creativity. Some of the most popular categories of paper crafts are scrapbooking, card making, and rubber stamping. Other types of paper crafts, such as collage art, Artist Trading Cards, art journaling, and paper-crafted home décor, are also gaining popularity. To begin, you will need a few basic supplies and some tips on combining colors.

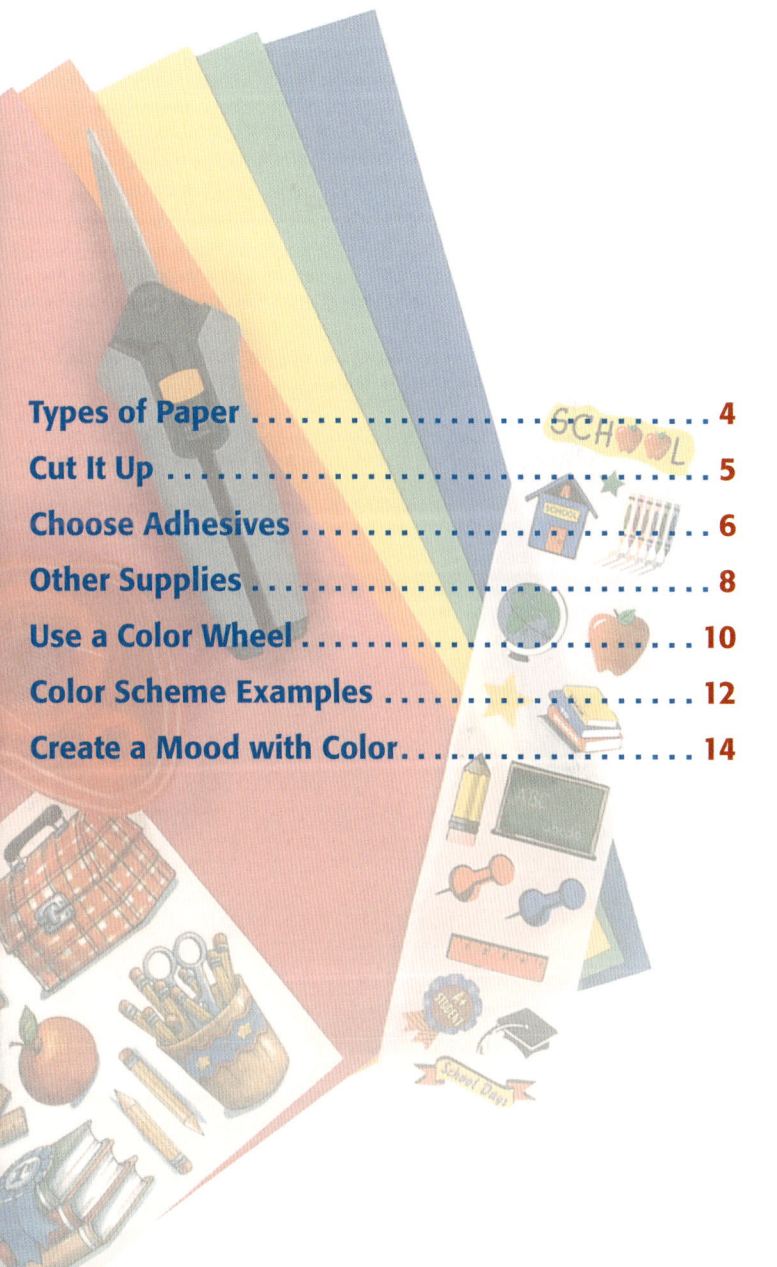

Types of Paper **4**
Cut It Up **5**
Choose Adhesives **6**
Other Supplies **8**
Use a Color Wheel **10**
Color Scheme Examples **12**
Create a Mood with Color........ **14**

Types of Paper

Paper crafting is, of course, all about the paper. The array of paper available is amazing and can be a bit overwhelming at first. Choosing paper appropriate for your specific project will be easier after this overview of paper types.

Cardstock is a paper crafting necessity. You can create greeting cards, mini-scrapbooks, gift tags, and more using only different colors of this heavyweight paper. An easy way to coordinate cardstock is to purchase it in monochromatic sets of different shades.

Patterned paper adds interest to your cardstock layers. This lighter-weight paper comes in every print imaginable. Pattern paper fills in the spots in your projects that may look a little too plain.

Specialty paper includes handmade paper, vellum, mulberry paper, metallics, and meshes. The translucent quality of vellum makes it perfect for layering. When you tear mulberry or handmade papers, you get a fuzzy edge that adds an interesting texture to your project. Just a small amount of metallic or mesh can add a significant level of texture and drama to a page.

Cut It Up

Trimming, cropping, and *edging* are all fancy words for cutting up things. Good scissors and a paper trimmer are a must. Shape cutters and punches make their respective tasks quicker and easier.

Scissors are a paper crafter's best friend. A good-quality pair of scissors with a nice sharp edge makes every paper task you do easier. Decorative scissors come in many different styles and can be used to add interest to the edges of greeting cards and other projects.

Paper trimmers are a must for cutting sheets of paper and for getting a straight edge when you crop or trim photos. A 12-inch trimmer enables you to cut any size of paper. You will find yourself pulling out your trimmer for almost all of your paper-craft projects.

Shape cutters and punches are used to cut paper and photos into a variety of shapes and designs. The most basic shape cutter can be used to cut circles and ovals of varying sizes. Punches come in every shape and size imaginable. Select some basic punches like circle, square, and tag shapes that you will use again and again.

Introduction to Paper Crafts

Choose Adhesives

Holding papers together is the job of adhesives. There are many different types and styles of adhesive, each of which is best for a specific type of paper crafting. Choosing the right one makes all the difference in how your project turns out.

TAPE RUNNERS

These versatile adhesive dispensers are the right choice for adhering paper and photos to cards, tags, journals, and scrapbook pages. Tape runners dispense clear sticky strips, white squares, or even little blue dots of adhesive.

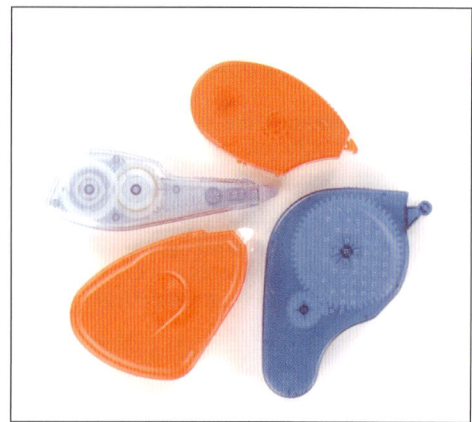

PHOTO TAPE, TACKY TAPE, AND FOAM SQUARES

These are specialty adhesives used for specific types of projects. Photo tape is perfect for making your own scrapbooks and tag albums. Sticky tape or tacky tape is great for adding embellishing stripes of glitter, sand, or beads. Double-sided foam adhesive attaches items to your projects while giving them a bit of lift for added dimension.

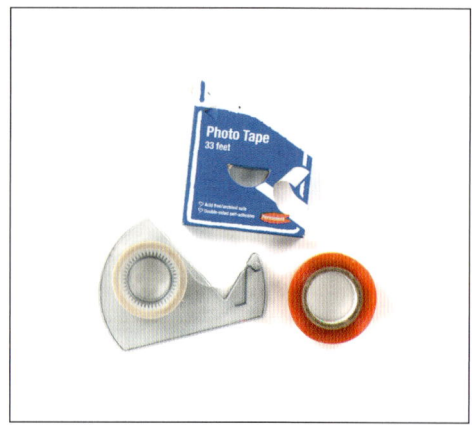

ADHESIVE DOTS

These super-sticky little dots come in a variety of sizes and thicknesses, and are exactly what you need to adhere dimensional items such as buttons, metal embellishments, and fabric and ribbon strips to your projects.

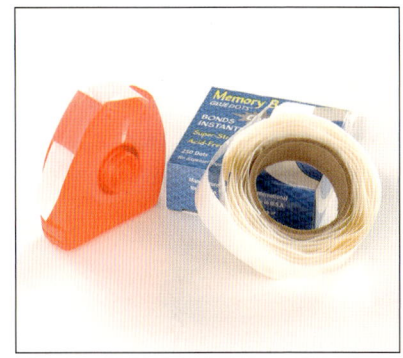

LIQUID GLUES AND GLUE PENS

You will use liquid glue on projects such as collage and decoupage. Liquid glues and glue pens are also good for metal embellishments and tiny items like letter die-cuts. Use liquid glues sparingly to avoid spillover.

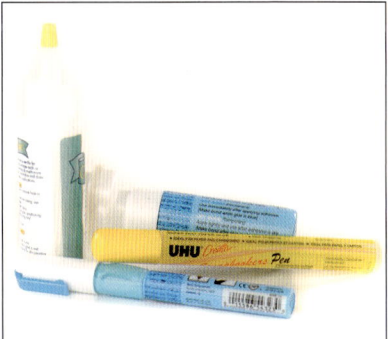

ADHESIVE MACHINES

Adhesive machines are the fastest way to adhere die-cuts to your projects. Simply insert an item into the machine, turn the crank or pull the strip, and out the other side come stickers. If you decide to use die-cut letters, an adhesive machine is a must.

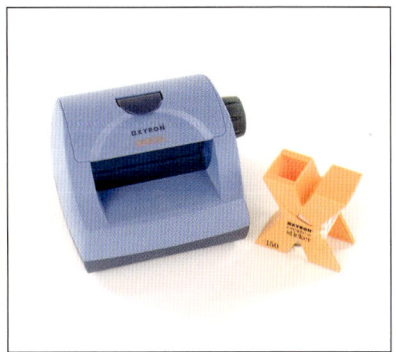

Introduction to Paper Crafts

Other Supplies

Along with the basics of paper and cutting supplies, many paper craft projects require a few additional tools. Specialty tools for specific crafts will be discussed in later chapters, but these are some basic items that you may want to add to your supply case.

TOOLS FOR LETTERING

A basic black pen will be your best friend when it comes to lettering on scrapbook pages and greeting cards. To add some interest to your lettering, you may want to invest in a set of permanent pens in a variety of colors. Metallic pens work well on dark papers. Your computer is also an invaluable tool for lettering.

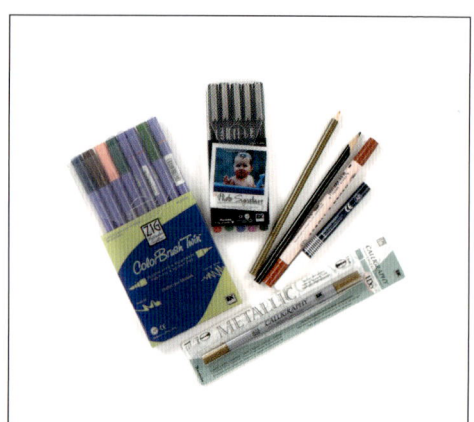

STAMPS AND STAMP PADS

Rubber stamps and stamp pads combine to help you add lettering and designs to your projects. You can also use stamps to apply color directly to paper. To begin, select stamp designs or alphabets that are versatile and can be used on a variety of projects.

PAINTS, CHALKS, AND METALLIC RUB-ON'S

Adding color to your paper-crafting projects can be done with craft paints, chalks, and rub-on's. Paint can be used with brushes or rubber stamps, while chalks and rub-on's are most commonly used to highlight smaller areas.

TEMPLATES AND STENCILS

Plastic templates can be used to create shapes and to guide you as you cut out paper letters. Brass stencils are used to make raised decorative surfaces on your projects—dry embossing. Both templates and stencils can be used in combination with paints, chalks, and rub-on's to add color in specific shapes.

Introduction to Paper Crafts 9

Use a Color Wheel

In your first art class in elementary school, you probably learned about the color wheel. This simple device, which demonstrates the relationship of colors to one another, is especially useful to paper crafters. The samples of scrapbook pages on p. 12–13 demonstrate the relationship of colors in some basic combinations. These same rules also apply in card making and other paper crafts.

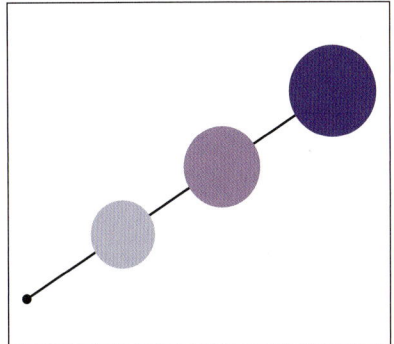

Monochromatic colors are varying shades of the same color, can complement most photos, and are easy to select.

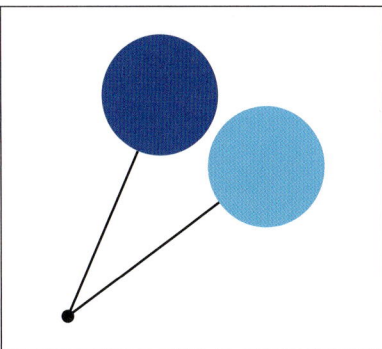

Analogous colors are two colors that are next to each other on the color wheel.

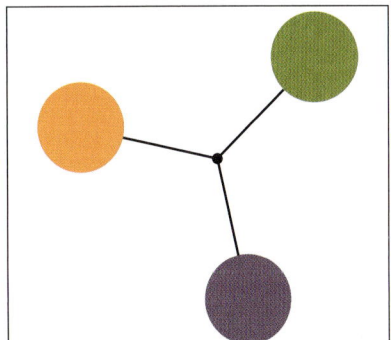

Triadic colors are any three colors that are exactly one-third of the color wheel away from each other.

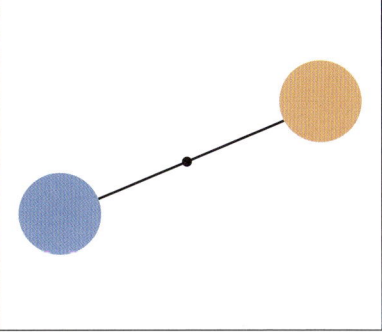

Complementary colors reside directly across from each other on the color wheel and can add extra "pop" to your design.

Introduction to Paper Crafts

Color Scheme Examples

MONOCHROMATIC

This scrapbook page layout uses varying shades of purple that accent the baby's bow. An advantage of monochromatic color schemes is that the colors tend to fade to the background, allowing the photos to be the main attraction.

ANALOGOUS

The scrapbook page shown here uses blue and blue-green as an analogous color scheme.

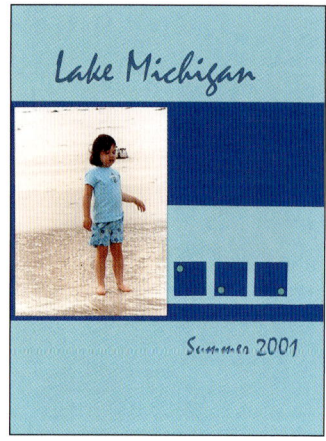

TRIADIC COLOR

In the scrapbook layout shown here, purple, green, and orange are used as a triadic color scheme. To give balance to the layout, one color (orange) is chosen as the dominant shade and the other two are used as accents.

COMPLEMENTARY

The scrapbook page layout shown here uses a complementary color combination of blue and orange. Matching the shades of the colors when you combine them is an important part of all color schemes. Light blue and light orange are used on this layout.

Create a Mood with Color

Color can help tell the story of your layout. Bright, warm colors reflect a playful party. Cool, calm colors create a quiet, reflective mood. Everything from scrapbook pages to party invitations will have a different mood based on the color combinations used to create them. The scrapbook page shown here uses neon shades of primary colors to make an exciting beach-themed layout.

At the Beach
Lindsey has always loved swimming, so it makes complete sense that one of her very favorite places is the beach.

This scrapbook page shows the exact same photos with a cool, monochromatic color scheme. Notice how the color choices affect the feel and mood of the layout.

At the Beach
Lindsey has always loved swimming, so it makes complete sense that one of her very favorite places is the beach.

chapter 2

Getting Started Scrapbooking

Scrapbooking is a hugely popular category of paper crafting. Preserving family, vacation, and heritage memories is a very rewarding hobby. To begin scrapbooking, take some time to understand the types of albums that are available to you. Once you have a scrapbook album picked out, a few simple tips will help you create your first scrapbook page.

Why Scrapbook? 18
Choose Your Album 20
Common Album Sizes 21
The Basics of a Layout 22
Make Your First Page 23
Mat a Photo 24
Matting Techniques 25
Create a Focal Point 26
Scrapbook Page Gallery 28

Why Scrapbook?

Understanding why scrapbooking is important to you and deciding what your purpose is in scrapbooking determine the types of supplies, embellishments, and album that you use.

PRESERVE YOUR PHOTOS

Many pictures that have been put into photo albums over the last 50 years have been damaged by the harsh chemicals used in the adhesives in those albums. Scrapbookers need to use photo-safe materials (paper, adhesives, and inks) that will not damage photos in order to preserve them for future generations.

SAVE YOUR MEMORIES

Photos without journaling are memories for only a short time. Soon the names, places, and event information are lost and only a photo remains. The heritage photos (family pictures from previous generations) shown here have no memories associated with them because the names and information about these people have been lost over time.

RECORD MAJOR EVENTS

Weddings, graduations, birthdays, holidays, and anniversaries are among the many life events that easily lend themselves to scrapbooking.

RESEARCH YOUR FAMILY HISTORY

Genealogy study and even just looking up the basics of your family tree can be the perfect time to start scrapbooking. Documenting this information in a scrapbook will allow future generations to benefit from the knowledge you have gleaned of your family's heritage.

REMEMBER THOSE PRECIOUS EVERYDAY MOMENTS

Not every photo you take will be of a major event in your life. Most of them will be the little things. These everyday pictures will be treasured in your scrapbooks for years to come.

Getting Started Scrapbooking 19

Choose Your Album

Scrapbooks come in a variety of styles and colors. Each style is defined by a distinctive binding method. Looking at the pros and cons of each style can help you choose which one is right for your project.

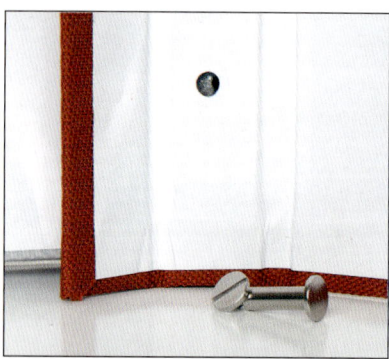

Post-bound albums are bound by screws and posts. The page protectors are bound into the album.

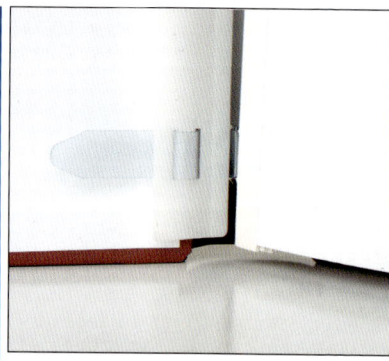

Strap-hinge albums are bound by a plastic strap that passes through staples in the edges of the pages.

Three-ring binding albums have a lot in common with classic three-ring office binders.

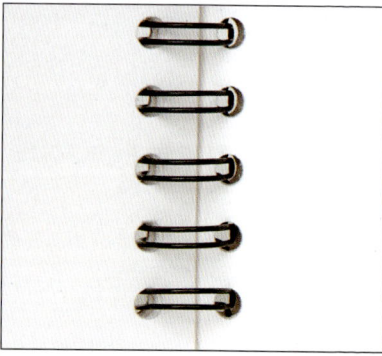

Spiral and book-bound albums are usually chosen for special projects and gift albums.

Common Album Sizes

The scrapbook project you are working on determines the size of album you need. The variety of sizes available will spark your creativity and get you thinking about all the different albums you could make for friends and family. The most common sizes of scrapbook albums are 12" × 12" and 8½" × 11".

12" x 12" albums are the most popular albums. The larger page size allows room for many photos and embellishments.

8½" x 11" albums are a good choice for more defined projects, such as school albums or children's scrapbooks.

6" x 6" and 8" x 8" albums are perfect for gift or theme scrapbooks.

Mini-books, or small specialty albums, are complete-in-a-weekend scrapbooks that come in many shapes and varieties.

Getting Started Scrapbooking

The Basics of a Layout

Scrapbook pages can be created in many styles with several different types of embellishments; however, they all break down into the same basic parts. Understanding the parts of a layout will guide you in creating your first page.

1. **Focal Point Photo:** Select one photo that tells the main story of the page.
2. **Supporting Photos:** These photos support the main photo and complete the story without taking the focus off of the focal point.
3. **Background Cardstock:** A solid sheet of color is used here as the foundation of the layout.
4. **Embellishments (Button and Cut-Out):** Simple decorations add to the theme of the page without distracting from the photos.
5. **Title:** A title defines the theme of the page.
6. **Journaling Box:** Journaling consists of the words that complete the story—the emotions behind the photos or simply the who, what, when, where, and why.

Make Your First Page

1. Gather the supplies that coordinate with your photos and your theme.

2. Decorate the background cardstock. Simple stripes are added here to break up the color and add visual interest.

3. Decide where to place the photos on the layout.
4. Add a title and journaling.
5. Add any desired embellishments. Pre-printed graphics, stickers, or dimensional decorations make finishing your page quick and easy.

Getting Started Scrapbooking 23

Mat a Photo

Matting a photo is simply creating a piece of cardstock that is slightly larger than the photo so that it leaves an even frame showing on all edges. Usually, a ⅛" cardstock "frame" is ideal. You may choose to leave ¼" or more showing to create a larger mat. You can measure the ⅛" space or simply eyeball it for greater speed and efficiency.

① Adhere your photo to a corner of the cardstock, leaving equal amounts showing on the two corner edges.

② Using a trimmer, cut along one of the two remaining sides, leaving ⅛" of cardstock showing around the photo.

③ Cut the final edge, making it equal to the previous three sides.

④ The photo now has a perfect mat and is ready to be placed on a scrapbook page.

Matting Techniques

MULTIPLE PHOTOS ON ONE MAT

A quick technique for matting photos is to mat several on one strip of cardstock. It takes a bit of measuring, but the time it saves in the end is worth it. The finished layout uses a strip of photos across the top of the scrapbook page matted on a single piece of black cardstock.

COMBO MATS

An alternate version of multiple photos on one mat is to combine a photo mat with other parts of the layout. In the example shown here, the photo mat includes the journaling box. Once again, this technique saves time. Another advantage is that it ties different parts of the layout together to create a cohesive page.

EMBELLISHED MATS

You can draw attention to a particular photo in a layout by embellishing the photo mat with a decorative border. Paper tearing in this example mimics the texture of the elephants in the photos.

Getting Started Scrapbooking   25

Create a Focal Point

Before: Great scrapbook pages catch the reader's eye. When planning a layout, remember that having a focal point, or a main photo, adds impact to your page. In this layout, each photo has equal importance, or weight, on the page. The eye has nowhere specific to land, which creates a visual jumble.

After: Select a photo that can be enlarged or cropped to give it maximum impact on the layout and to give your reader's eye something to focus on. This photo is your focal point. Here the scrapbook page has a clear focal point photo. Supporting photos have been narrowed down to just the best ones needed to tell the story of the page.

Mikhail loves sports. In Spring 2005, he started soccer and can't get enough of it. His natural abilities are shining through, we can't wait to see how his interests grow and change as we watch him grow-up.

PRACTICE
makes Perfect

Getting Started Scrapbooking 27

Scrapbook Page Gallery

Title: "Charlie in the Snow" by Jennifer Foster. **Materials Used:** Patterned paper – Daisy D's; Cardstock – Die Cuts With a View; Label – DYMO; "snow" letters – Scrapworks; Snowflake – Making Memories; Beads – Stampin' Up; Wire – Artistic Wire; Corner punch – EK Success; Brads – Bazzill; Flower punch – EK Success; Fonts – Creating Keepsakes; Die-cut letter – QuiKutz; Glitter.

Title: "Back to the Grind Stone" by Tracey Eller. **Materials Used**: Paper – Bazzill; Rub-on's – My Mind's Eye and Making Memories; Ink – Ranger; Clips – Creative Impressions; Tiles, rings, and anchors – Junkitz.

CONTINUED ON NEXT PAGE

Getting Started Scrapbooking

Scrapbook Page Gallery (continued)

Title: "Navy" by Jennifer Schmidt. **Materials Used:** Printed paper – Fiskars; Photo corners – Fiskars and Creative Memories; Eyelets – Karen Foster Design; 3-D stickers – K&Company.

Title: *"Amaizeing Adventure" by Michon Kessler.* ***Materials Used:*** *Patterned papers – Daisy D's and K&Company; Vellum, brads, and textured paper – Provo Craft; Antique brads, vellum tag, definition, and metal plaque – Making Memories; Sticker – Melissa Francis.*

chapter 3

Card Making Basics

Sending a greeting card is a way to tell someone special "Happy Birthday," "Thank You," "I Miss You," and so much more. These sentiments are even more profound when you use your paper-crafting supplies and techniques to make the card yourself. With just a few tips and techniques, you will be sending off handmade greetings for every occasion.

Envelope Sizes 34
Scoring and Folding 35
Make Your Own Envelopes 36
Photo Greeting Cards 38
Match Book Invitations 40
File Folder Cards 42
Make a Library Pocket Card 44
Window Cards 46
Pop-Up Cards 49
Dry Embossing Cards and Envelopes 52
Birthday Card Organizer 54
Recipe Book 57
Card Gallery 58

Envelope Sizes

The quickest way to begin making your own cards is by starting with pre-made envelopes. You can purchase envelopes in a wide variety of sizes and colors to match your card projects. This chart shows the most common sizes of rectangular envelopes that are available, the size to trim your cardstock to fit within each envelope, and the size of the finished card.

Envelope Sizes

Common Rectangular Envelope Sizes in Inches	Cut Cardstock to This Size in Inches	Finished Folded Card Size in Inches
Common Invitation and Card Envelope Sizes		
A2: 4 3/8 x 5 3/4	8 1/2 x 5 1/2	4 1/8 x 5 1/2
A6: 4 3/4 x 6 1/2	9 x 6 1/4	4 1/2 x 6 1/4
A7: 5 1/2 x 7 1/4	10 x 7	5 x 7
A9: 5 3/4 x 8 3/4	11 x 8 1/2	5 1/2 x 8 1/2
Common Letter and Business Envelope Sizes		
#6: 3 3/4 x 6 1/2	7 x 6 1/4	3 1/2 x 6 1/4
#10: 4 1/4 x 9 1/2	8 x 9 1/4	4 x 9 1/4

FAQ

I want to make my own invitations and cards but I don't have a lot of time. Any tips to help make the process faster?

Before you start putting your cards together, gather all of your supplies and cut all of your pieces. Now you can set everything up in an assembly line so that each invitation or greeting card only takes a few seconds to complete.

Scoring and Folding

Two basic techniques in card making are scoring and folding. You will most likely want to use a heavier-weight paper such as cardstock when making your greeting cards, and therefore scoring before you fold will give you much more precise fold lines. Folding with a bone folder presses the fold neatly and cleanly into the cardstock.

Scoring can be done using a scoring blade attachment, which is available for many types of paper trimmers. You can also score your cardstock as shown here using a simple embossing tool and a straight edge or ruler.

Folding is something that you can easily do without tools; however, a bone folder allows you to press folds into cardstock, creating tight creases. The result is a more professional-looking edge.

Card Making Basics

Make Your Own Envelopes

If you want more flexibility in envelope sizes, or in the color and even the pattern printed on your envelopes, you may want to make your own. Using the template provided in the Appendix, making your own envelopes is a relatively simple process.

① Copy or scan and print out the envelope template on p. 200, resizing it until the rectangle in the middle is slightly bigger than the card you will be inserting into the finished envelope. Cut out the template and trace it onto the back of your choice of paper or cardstock.

② Cut out the traced envelope, score, and fold on the fold lines. You may want to use a corner rounder on some of the sharp corners for a finished look.

③ Add double-stick tape to close up the sides and bottom of the envelope.

④ If using patterned paper or dark-colored cardstock to make the envelope, be sure to print white address labels for mailing.

TIP

By adjusting the size of the envelopes and the paper used to make them, this template can serve many uses. You can make tiny gift-card-size envelopes for holiday gift giving. You can make vellum envelopes for use on scrapbook pages or in mini-books. You can also coordinate the look of the envelope to match the greeting card that will go inside of it.

Card Making Basics

Photo Greeting Cards

Holiday cards sent annually to family and friends are much more personal when they include a photo that shows how much your family has grown over the last year. Making your own photo greeting cards is also a quick and simple way to share pictures for any occasion.

1. Cut solid cardstock to fit in the envelopes that you will be using to send the cards.

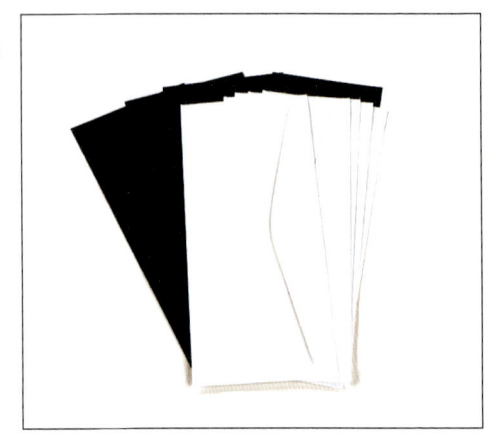

2. Trim the photo to fit on the card, leaving room for journaling.

❸ Print journaling on the cardstock, and trim to fit on the card.

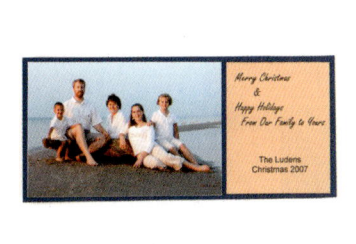

❹ Add flat embellishments such as punches and stickers to complete the card.

The finished card looks both elegant and handmade. Use this same technique to make cards for graduation or new baby announcements.

Card Making Basics

Match Book Invitations

The basic shape of a match book can become the perfect form for invitations and greeting cards. The cover is decorated to match the theme of the occasion, and when the book is flipped open, it reveals room for event information.

① Using the pattern found on p. 201 as a guide, cut a cover and inside page for your match book.

② Score the match book cover on all fold lines to ensure crisp and even folds.

③ Fold the cover and press the folds with a bone folder.

④ Insert the inside page into the book cover, and staple in place, as shown.

5 Embellish the outside of the cover as desired, and add event information on the inside page. The completed invitation is a charming way to let your guests know that you are having a party.

Match books can also be used on scrapbook pages to hold extra photos or journaling. The page shown here has a row of match book journaling boxes across the bottom.

TIP

The match book shape can also be used to create mini-books. Simply by increasing the number of pages inside the cover, you have a small book that can hold photos, memorabilia, and journaling. As the thickness of the book increases, you may decide to use brads or eyelets as fasteners across the bottom in place of staples.

Card Making Basics 41

File Folder Cards

File folders are not just for offices anymore. The basic shape of a classic file folder is perfect for card making and for use on scrapbook pages.

1. Trace the file folder pattern from p. 203 onto a piece of cardstock. You can also scan the pattern into your computer and print it directly on the cardstock.

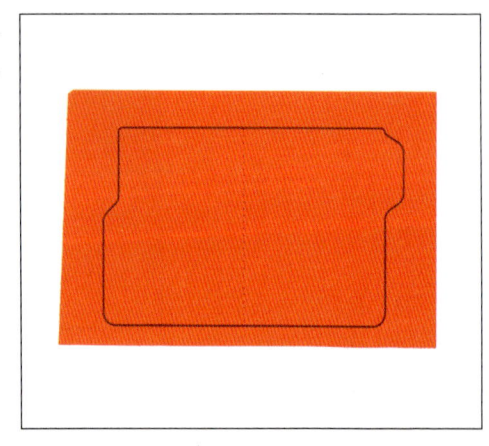

2. Cut out the file folder card, score, and fold it.

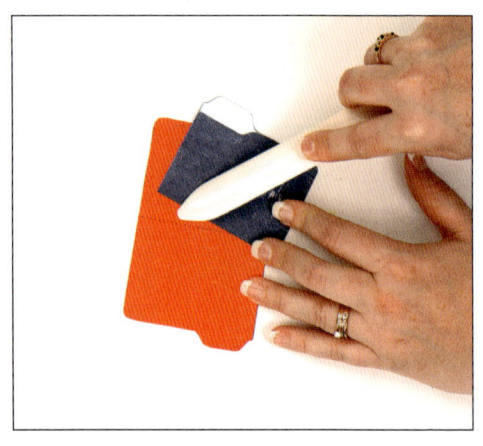

Thank You Card: File folders work for almost any theme. This thank you card with beautiful stripes, florals, and polka dots is sure to express your gratitude.

Baby Announcement: You can even use a file folder card for announcements. This card could hold a photo of a precious new baby. Send these to all of your friends, and they will be impressed with your new addition and your crafting skills.

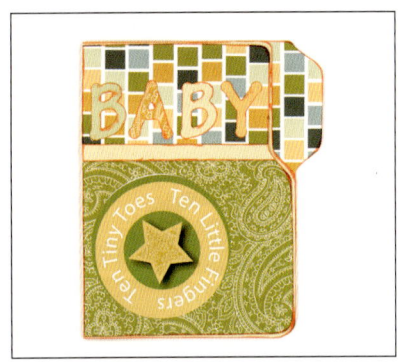

Journaling Folder: File folders on scrapbook pages allow you to add hidden journaling or extra photos to your pages.

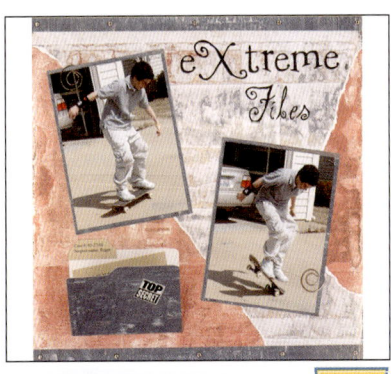

Card Making Basics 43

Make a Library Pocket Card

1. To begin, cut a strip of double-sided, patterned, heavy-weight paper or cardstock to the width of your finished card. The example shown here is 4¼" wide by 9¾" long.

2. Fold up the bottom of the strip, leaving 1½" showing at the top. To achieve the look of a library pocket, you may want to use a corner-rounder punch to round off the top two corners of the strip.

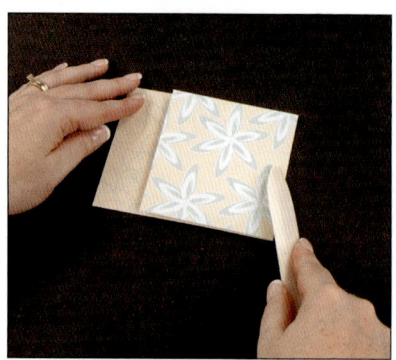

3. Add double-sided adhesive strips to each side of the folded piece, creating a pocket.

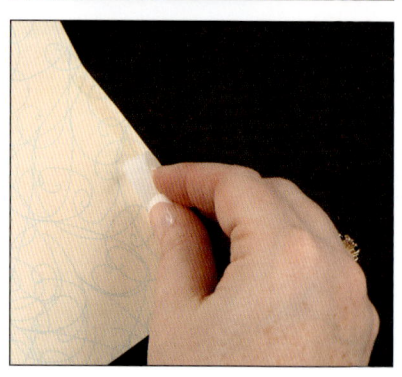

④ Cut a piece of cardstock to mat your invitation information and add it to the pocket.

⑤ Embellish the finished invitation as desired. On the bridal shower invitation shown here, die-cut letters indicating the bride's and groom's initials adorn the front. A flower cut from matching patterned paper and accented with a self-adhesive acrylic gem finishes off the invitation.

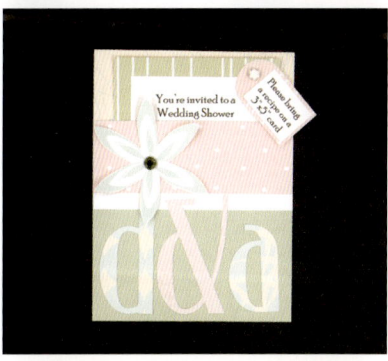

Library card pockets are also perfect for scrapbook pages. The pocket can be decorated with a title or photo on the front, and the inside can hold a journaling card.

Card Making Basics 45

Window Cards

Window cards have a cut-out in the cover of the card that looks through to the inside. The size and shape of the cut-out along with the embellishments on the card give you a huge range of creative possibilities.

① To begin, cut out, score, and fold a basic rectangular card. Also cut a piece of coordinating cardstock that is ¼" smaller in size in both directions than the cover of the card.

② Using square punches, punch out two squares from scrap paper (one slightly smaller than the other).

③ Adhere the larger punched square to the piece of coordinating cardstock exactly where you would like your window to be located on the card. Turn the punch used to make that square upside down so that you can see where you are punching. Line up the opening with the square scrap and punch a window in your cardstock.

④ Adhere the cardstock to the cover of the card, being sure to center it all the way around. Stick the second (smaller) square in the window opening exactly where you want the finished window to be centered.

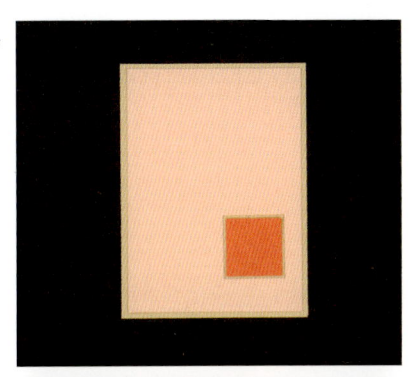

⑤ Using the smaller-size square punch, once again turn it upside down so you can see where you are punching. Punch out over the scrap square of paper.

⑥ The finished basic window card has a matted window that shows through to the inside. It is now ready to be embellished to match the occasion.

CONTINUED ON NEXT PAGE

Window Cards (continued)

This window card has been embellished with patterned paper, sticker letters, fish buttons, and a fish charm to make a pool party invitation.

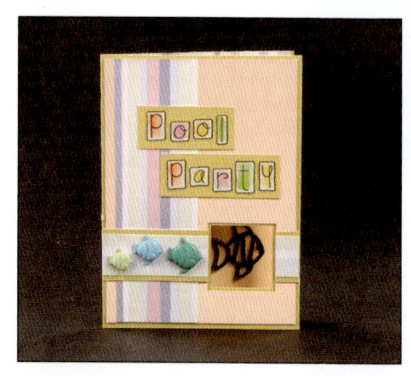

This beautiful Thanksgiving card was made using a self-adhesive frame around the window and a wide piece of ribbon for added dimension.

Multiple window openings can be used to display a stamped word, such as the word "LOVE" shown here. In addition to multiple windows, you may also want to try windows in different shapes, such as circles or hearts.

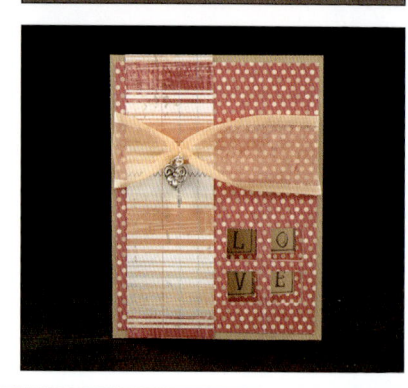

Pop-Up Cards

Pop-up cards have more dimension than any other type of greeting card. Even though they look complicated, with a simple pattern and a few step-by-step instructions, you will have a blast making cards that pop up.

1. To begin, cut and score a basic cardstock card. Also cut a mat for this card that is ¼" larger than the card on all sides. Do not adhere the card to the mat until instructed to do so.

2. Scan or copy the pop-up card pattern found on p. 205, resizing it to make it fit your card. Transfer the pattern to your card by pressing firmly with a scoring tool, marking all cut lines and fold lines on the card.

CONTINUED ON NEXT PAGE

Card Making Basics

Pop-Up Cards
(continued)

3. Use a craft knife and straight edge to carefully cut on all of the cut lines as indicated on the pattern.

4. Fold the card, popping out the pieces as shown. Fold each of the pop-up pieces in the opposite direction from the card as it closes. You may want to press it closed and open it again a couple of times so that the paper "learns" the folds.

5. Adhere the card to the mat, being careful to not place any adhesive behind the sections that will pop up. Your basic pop-up card is complete and ready to be embellished as you desire.

The baby announcement card shown here has been embellished with hand-cut arrows and a title sticker. The arrows around the photo were the perfect place to record the baby's name, weight, and length.

You can also use paper piecing to embellish your pop-up cards. The patterns for the banner, cake, candle, and party hat shown here can be found on p. 206.

FAQ

I would like to use some stickers to embellish the pop-up sections of my card. How can I use stickers without them sticking to the back of the card?

The easiest way to use stickers on your pop-up card is to adhere them to an extra piece of cardstock and then cut them out. They will not be sticky and they will also have the thickness required to stand up on the pop-up.

Card Making Basics

Dry Embossing Cards and Envelopes

With a few special supplies, you can add an extra touch to your cards and envelopes. Dry embossing creates a raised edge to give some added texture to any project.

① Gather an embossing tool, a light box, a brass stencil, masking tape, some cardstock, and patterned paper.

② Use a piece of masking tape to temporarily adhere the brass stencil to the light box.

③ Lay a piece of paper over the stencil, upside down. The light will show through the paper, making the stencil visible.

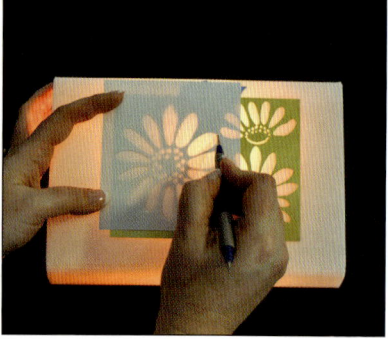

④ Using the embossing tool, press gently to outline the inside edges of each part of the stencil design.

⑤ When you lift up the piece of paper, it will be embossed with the stencil design. You can now cut out the piece, being sure to cut just outside of the raised lines.

⑥ Adhere the completed dry-embossed pieces to a cardstock card to finish your design. You may want to use double-sided adhesive foam tape to give your pieces even more dimension.

⑦ You can also dry emboss part of the stencil design onto the flap of your envelope for an extra special touch.

Card Making Basics

Birthday Card Organizer

Making cards ahead of time will help you be ready for birthdays throughout the year. Keeping your handmade cards organized and keeping track of birthdates can be easily handled by this adorable organizer that you can make yourself.

1 Cut 2 pieces of chipboard for covers to 8¼" x 6½". Cut 4 pieces of patterned paper or cardstock the same size as the covers. You will also need 6 sheets of heavyweight 12" x 12" patterned paper for the inside pages.

2 Cover the chipboard pieces with patterned paper or cardstock. A glue stick works well for attaching paper to chipboard.

③ Fold the bottom 4" up toward the top on each of 6 sheets of 12" x 12" heavyweight patterned paper.

④ Fold each sheet in half, creating a page that is 8" x 6" and has a pocket on the front and back.

⑤ Bind the covers to the pages. You can do this yourself by punching holes in each layer and inserting rings, or you can have it professionally spiral-bound at your local copy center or office supply store.

⑥ Add a tab to each page, marking them with the months of the year—2 months per tab.

CONTINUED ON NEXT PAGE

Card Making Basics

Birthday Card Organizer *(continued)*

Use a calendar stamp to add a reminder card to each page if desired.

Embellish the cover using ribbon, flowers, or other decorations.

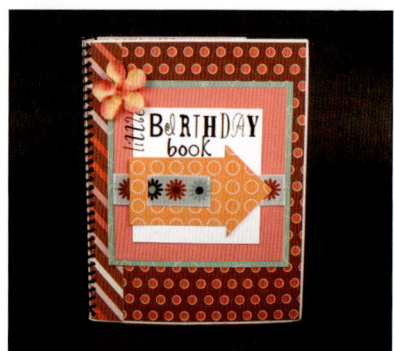

Fill pockets with handmade birthday cards.

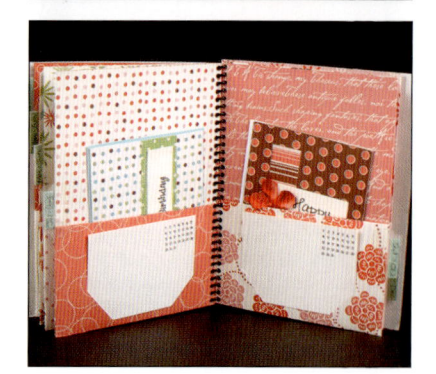

Recipe Book

The Birthday Card Organizer book can be embellished for other themes and occasions. As shown here, the book becomes a treasure trove of family recipes, perfect for a bridal shower gift.

The outside of the book has been embellished with a title tag, stickers, and rubber stamping. When binding this book, a clear acetate cover sheet is bound as the first page, helping to protect the book during many years of use in the kitchen.

The inside pages are tabbed with titles such as Appetizers, Main Dishes, Side Dishes, Vegetables, Desserts, and Breads. The pockets are filled with coordinating 3" x 5" cards on which guests can print recipes for the bride.

Card Making Basics

Card Gallery

BIRTHDAY CARDS

Title: *"Happy Birthday" by Beth Price.* ***Materials Used:*** *Papers – Scenic Route Paper Co., and a button.*

Title: *"Happy Birthday" by Jennifer Schmidt.* ***Materials Used:*** *Pattern paper and stickers – Making Memories; Flower – Heidi Swapp.*

Card Making Basics 59

Card Gallery (continued)

THANK YOU CARDS

Title: "Many Thanks" by Rebecca Ludens. *Materials Used:* Patterned paper – Provo Craft and solid brown paper – Li'l Davis Designs; Flower and brad – Hot Off The Press; Font Arial.

Title: *"Thank U" by Jennifer Schmidt.* ***Materials Used:*** *Patterned paper and sticker – Mustard Moon; Rub-on's – Making Memories; Ribbon – May Arts.*

Card Making Basics

chapter 4

Book Making

Making your own mini-books is an important part of paper crafting. Your books can be used to showcase your other paper-craft techniques, such as quilling (see Chapter 6), collage, art journaling, scrapbooking, and so on. These little books also make fabulous gifts for any occasion.

Basic Mini-Book.................................. **64**
Baby's First Year Mini-Book...................... **68**
Mini-Book on a Scrapbook Page.................... **69**
Envelope Book.................................... **70**
Travel-Themed Envelope Book...................... **73**
Accordion Book................................... **74**
Paper Bag Book................................... **78**
Friends Paper Bag Book........................... **81**
Container Books.................................. **82**

Basic Mini-Book

This basic mini-book is the perfect way to begin making your own books. It makes a wonderful small scrapbook gift or journal. You can also use it on a scrapbook page to give yourself more room for photos and journaling.

The books shown here would make a great photo brag book for your purse. You could also embellish the covers of these little books to personalize them. You could create one of these books to use as your first art journal.

1. To begin creating your first book, cut a piece of chipboard (the cardboard on the back of a pad of paper) into two pieces. Each piece should measure 6" x 4½".

② Choose a piece of printed paper for the cover of the book. Cut this piece to 7" x 10½". Adhere the chipboard pieces to the back of the cover paper, leaving ½" between them and making sure that equal amounts of the paper are showing on all sides.

③ Fold each corner in toward the center of the chipboard as shown, and glue in place.

④ Fold the remaining edges of the paper around the chipboard and use photo tape to adhere them firmly into place.

CONTINUED ON NEXT PAGE

Book Making 65

Basic Mini-Book
(continued)

5 Cut two pieces of ribbon each 9" long. Adhere each piece to the back of the chipboard as shown, using photo tape.

6 Make the inside pages by cutting at least three, or as many as seven, pieces of cardstock to 8½" x 5½".

7 Fold each piece exactly in half and press with a bone folder to create a nice, sharp crease.

⑧ Adhere each folded piece back to back with another piece as shown. When complete, they look like the pages of a book.

⑨ Adhere the pages to the inside of the completed cover, using photo tape to hold them firmly in place.

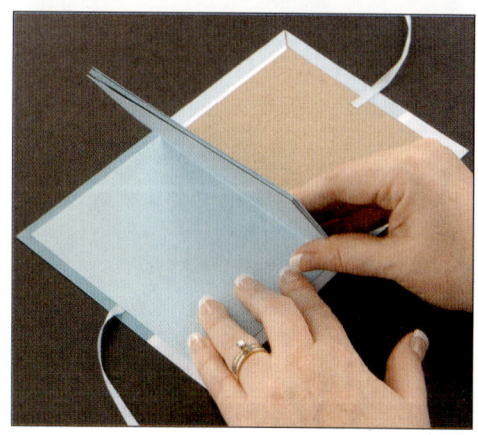

TIP

You can increase the number of pages in the book; however, you will want to make the cover cardstock slightly bigger and leave a little more space between the cardstock covers to accommodate the added thickness.

Book Making

Baby's First Year Mini-Book

After you complete the book, you can pick a theme and add photos, journaling, and simple embellishments. Because the theme for this book is "Baby's First Year," the book has dated tabs that mark the months.

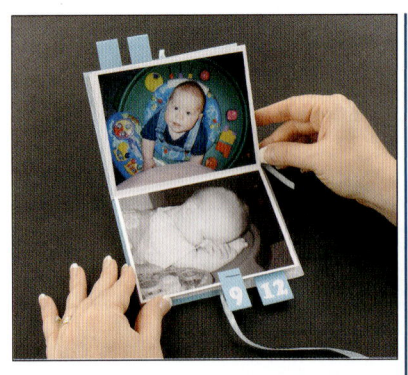

1 Add photos to the book by trimming a 4" x 6" photo slightly to fill the page. Smaller photos can be matted to fill the page.

2 Create tabs for the book by cutting strips of paper or cardstock that are 3½" long x ½" wide. Fold each strip in half.

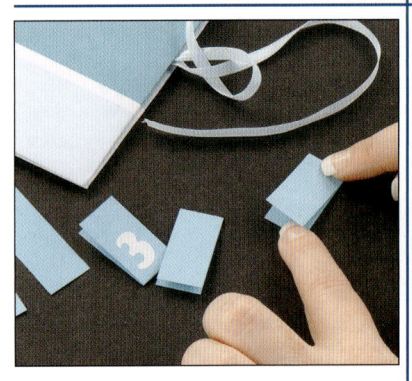

3 Add a sticker or rub-on number to the tab.

4 Staple each tab to the edge of an album page.

Mini-Book on a Scrapbook Page

To use a mini-book on a scrapbook page, all you need to do is adhere it to your page with photo tape. You may need to add some chipboard to the back of the scrapbook page to give it added stability to hold the weight of the book. On this layout, ultrasound photos of the baby are housed inside a mini-book.

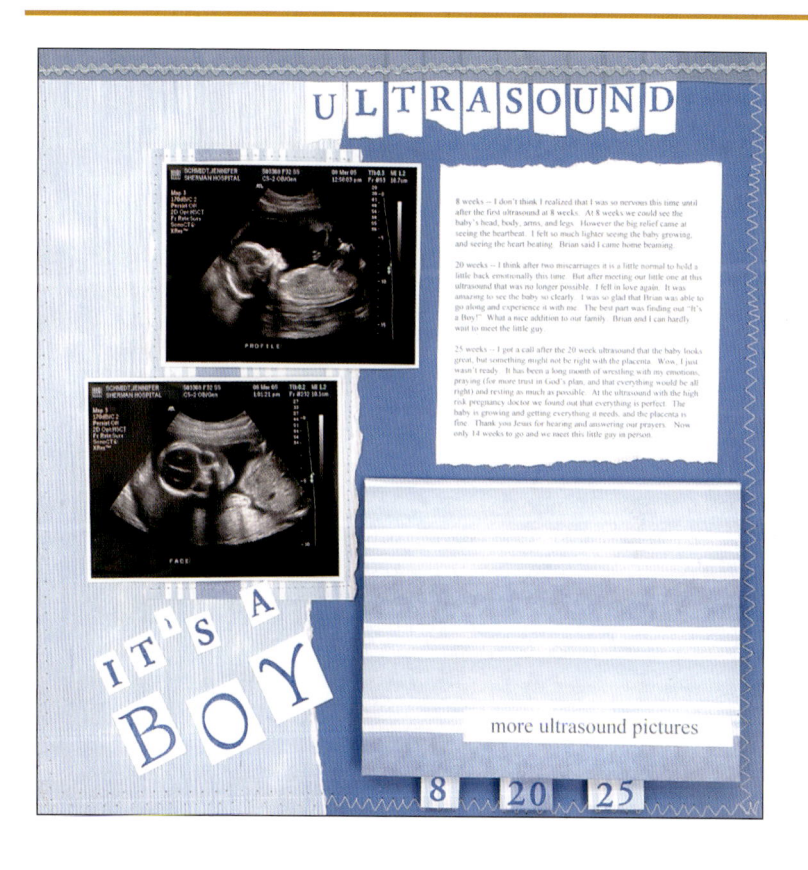

Book Making

Envelope Book

Envelopes come in a variety of sizes, shapes, and colors. By using these often-overlooked items to create a scrapbook, your pages automatically have pockets to contain journaling tags or precious memorabilia. The book shown here would be perfect for pictures to help you remember a weekend at the beach.

You can see that by following simple steps, envelopes can become an adorable mini-book that can hold photos, memorabilia, journaling, tags, cards, and more.

1. Begin by gathering supplies that coordinate with the theme of your mini-book. Here you can see envelopes with tags, patterned papers, a charm, ribbon, colored string, rub-on's, and photos.

2 For this project you need an odd number of envelopes. You can make the book as large as you want. Select envelopes that are the size, shape, and color you desire for your theme.

3 Adhere the flap of one envelope to the bottom edge of the next. Continue until they are all attached in a long chain. Fan-fold the chain so that it closes in a neat stack.

4 If the flap on the final envelope contains adhesive, cover it with a coordinating piece of paper to prevent humidity from causing it to stick to the book in the future.

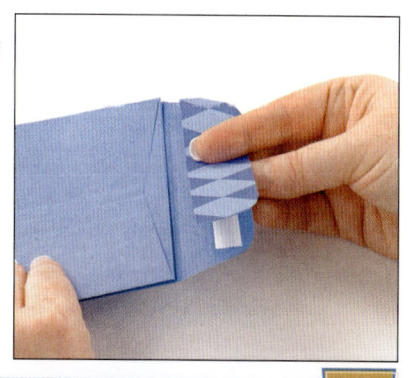

CONTINUED ON NEXT PAGE

Book Making

Envelope Book
(continued)

5 Trim your photos slightly so that they will fit on each page of the book.

6 Add journaling or memorabilia to tags that you have cut to fit inside each envelope.

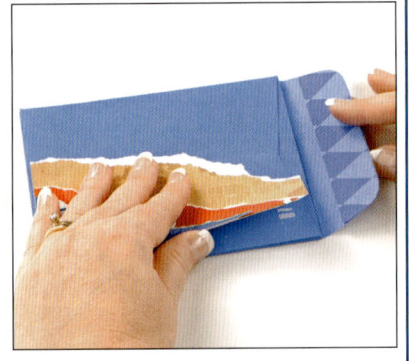

7 To decorate the cover, tear the patterned paper for texture and adhere to the front as a base. You could also add a photo.

8 Finish the book cover with a rub-on title. Tie a charm around the first envelope with a piece of colored string. Tie a piece of ribbon around the book to use as a closure.

Travel-Themed Envelope Book

The book shown here is a travel journal of a family's trip to Russia to adopt a child. An envelope book works perfectly as a travel journal because you have pockets for memorabilia, receipts, foreign money, and other items you may pick up on your trip.

① **Optional:** Ink the pages of the book to create an old-world look.

② When adding photos, you can use rub-on's to add words and titles right on top of the pictures.

③ Add tickets and other memorabilia to both the pages and the tags tucked inside each page.

④ Finish the book cover by inking and tearing a piece of patterned paper and adding a rub-on title and travel-themed words.

Book Making 73

Accordion Book

These exciting mini-books pop open to display photos, journaling, and small embellishments. The intricate design looks much more difficult to create than it really is.

Accordion books make great gifts, and the colors and papers can be coordinated to go with any theme. A matching ribbon is used as a closure on the finished book.

1. Cut two pieces of chipboard into 4½" squares and two pieces of patterned paper into 5½" squares for the cover of the book. You also need three 8" square pieces of cardstock and a 16" piece of ribbon.

❷ Cover the chipboard pieces with the two paper pieces intended for the cover by adhering the chipboard to the back center of the paper, trimming the corners, and folding over and gluing the edges.

❸ Adhere a piece of ribbon at least 16" long across the back of one of the cover pieces.

❹ Score three lines on each of the 8" squares, as shown here.

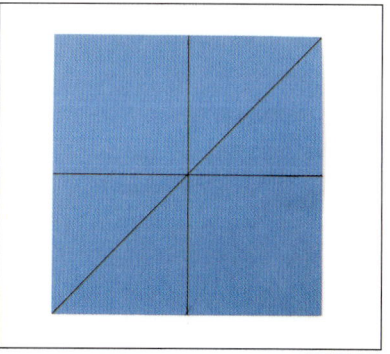

CONTINUED ON NEXT PAGE

Book Making 75

Accordion Book
(continued)

5 Papers with different shades front and back are shown here to make it easier to see the construction of the album. Fold on each of the three scored lines and open.

6 Fold each square into a smaller square by creating mountain folds along the diagonal score line. Bring these folds together toward the center of the square.

7 Finish the fold by pressing the two smaller squares together.

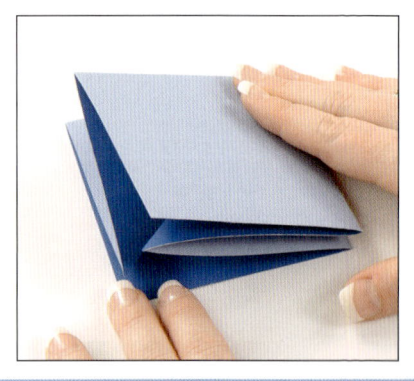

8 Fold all three squares in this manner to create three folded pieces that look like this.

9 Turn the center piece over so that you can overlap the small squares on each piece. Adhere these squares together.

10 Use photo tape to secure the folded pages to the insides of the book covers, being sure to center them on the back of each cover. The ribbon is used to secure the book closed.

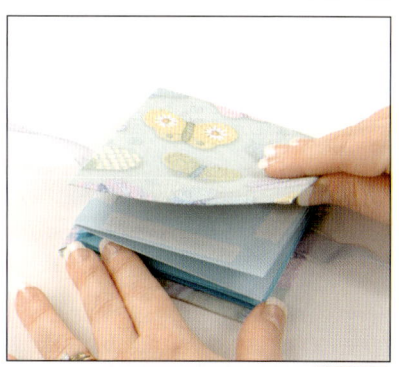

Book Making

Paper Bag Book

Once you start thinking about things that you can use in book making, you never know what you might come up with. Paper lunch bags, for example, can become an adorable mini-book. Because paper bags are not necessarily acid-free, be sure to use copies if you place photos in this book.

You can make paper bag books for any theme. This gorgeous anniversary-theme book details the "10 Things I Love About You After 10 Years." The pages are decorated with a cohesive color scheme of black, white, and red.

Each pair of pages in this album is decorated with a number that reflects the "10 Things," plus one or more photos that follow the theme. Each opening in the paper bags has tags slipped into it that allow extra room for journaling.

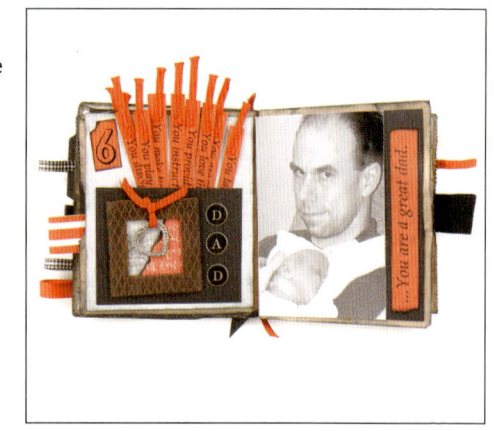

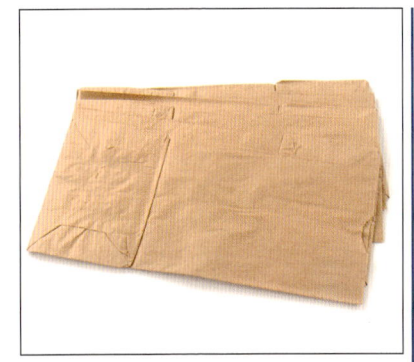

① Gather six paper lunch bags. Stack the bags right-side up with the ends of every other bag going in opposite directions.

② Ink the edges of all six bags. This step is much easier to complete before you finish assembling the book.

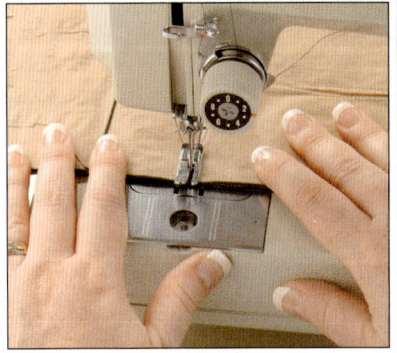

③ Fold the bags in half to crease the center line. Use a sewing machine to sew down the center of the bags.

④ Cut a strip of printed paper to 5¼" x 4". Adhere this strip of paper to the back of the stack of pages. Center the strip over the sewn line.

CONTINUED ON NEXT PAGE

Book Making 79

Paper Bag Book *(continued)*

5 Punch holes for eyelets ½" apart down one side of the center strip. Set eyelets in each of these holes.

6 Fold the book closed. Use a pen to mark through the eyelets to the pages beneath to indicate where you need to place the eyelets for the other side.

7 Open the book, punch holes at the pen marks, and set the eyelets in the holes.

8 Close the book. Tie lengths of ribbon through the holes to attach the front to the back of the book and hold everything in place.

Paper Crafts VISUAL Quick Tips

Friends Paper Bag Book

Paper bags do not have to be inked and chalked. They can, instead, have clean lines and bright colors. This "Friends" book shows how paper bag mini-books can be decorated with pink and purple to highlight photos of little girls.

Extra-large paint strips from the paint department of a home center are inserted into the bag openings as journaling tags. A small piece of ribbon attached to the tag makes each tag easier to remove from the book. The cover is embellished with silk flowers and mini-brads.

The inside of the book details what makes sisters such good friends. The pages are filled with photos of the girls and quotes about the special relationship shared by sisters.

Book Making

Container Books

Mini-books can be made more durable by encasing them in containers. Mint tins, CD cases, and cigar boxes can all be turned into container books. Dies used with Sizzix die-cutting machines come in clear plastic boxes that are perfect cases for container books.

The book shown here has 14 page sides that can be decorated with photos, journaling, and embellishments. The theme for this book is bringing home a new baby.

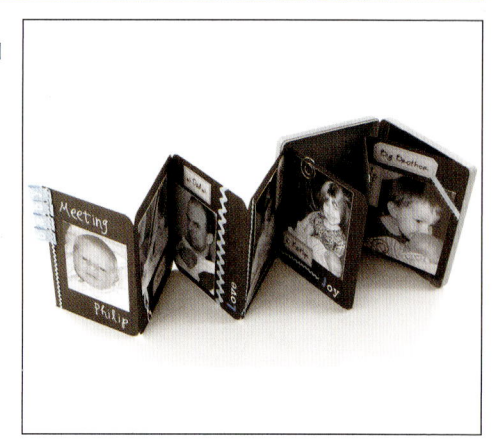

The outside of the container holding the book is also decorated with rub-on's, stickers, ribbon, and charms to match the theme.

1. Start with a plastic case. Here, a Sizzix die case for larger dies is used; it is approximately 5" x 5½" in size. Spray-paint the outside of the case and let it dry completely. Embellish the dry cover as desired.

2. Cut three 5" x 12" strips of cardstock.

3. Use photo tape to attach the end of each strip to the next one to create one strip of cardstock almost 36" long.

CONTINUED ON NEXT PAGE

Book Making 83

Container Books *(continued)*

④ Score lines every 4½" down the strip of cardstock and fold on these lines in an accordion-folded pattern, back and forth.

⑤ Use a corner-rounder punch to round off the corners at each folded edge.

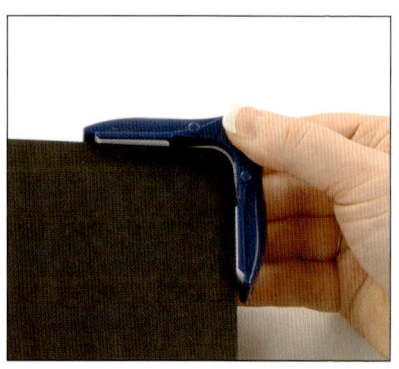

⑥ Use photo tape to attach the back page to the inside of the bottom of the painted case.

7. Decorate the first page with a photo that sets the theme of the album. Here the book is about family members meeting a new baby, so the baby photo is the focal point of the cover.

8. The inside pages are simply embellished with ribbon, brads, and tags that have the name of each family member. The photo on each page shows that person holding the new baby.

TIP

When spray-painting plastic boxes and metal tins, you will want to check with your local craft store to find paints that are appropriate for those surfaces. You can also experiment with different types of finishes such as metallic and stone-look spray paints to give your container books a one-of-a-kind look.

Book Making

chapter 5

Stamping

Stamping is a technique that can carry over into almost every form of paper crafting. You can stamp on scrapbook pages, greeting cards, mini-books, and even home décor. The basic techniques are simple, but your creativity can take stamping to extraordinary levels of artistry.

Types of Stamps **88**
Ink Pads and Cleaners **90**
Stamping Lettering **92**
Stamping with Bleach **94**
Pieced Stamping **96**
Double Stamping **98**
Heat Embossing **100**
Embellishing Stamping **102**

Types of Stamps

To begin stamping, you will, of course, need some stamps. You may be surprised to discover that stamps come in a variety of types. Rubber stamps mounted on wooden blocks are now just one of many kinds of stamps you can purchase.

Many rubber stamps still come mounted on wood blocks. The wood gives the stamps stability, making it easy to stamp a crisp, clean image.

For easy storage, some rubber stamps now come with a magnetic backing and are unmounted. You can store hundreds of stamps in one three-ring binder. You can even retro-fit magnet backings to your old rubber stamps. You will also need a collection of coordinating magnetic-backed wood blocks that can be used with all of your magnetic stamps.

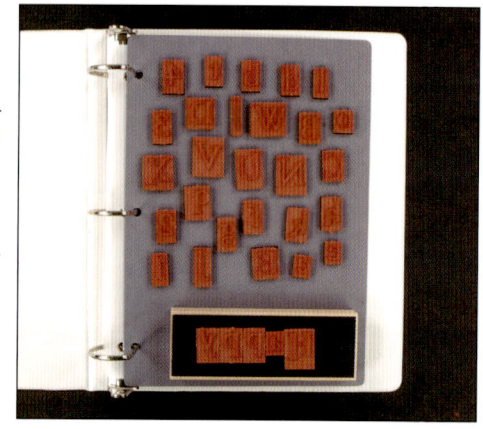

Acrylic stamps are clear and come on flat sheets for storage. To use acrylic stamps, you need acrylic blocks in a variety of sizes to accommodate all of your stamps. The huge benefit of acrylic is that you can see through the block and stamp to line up your image as you stamp it.

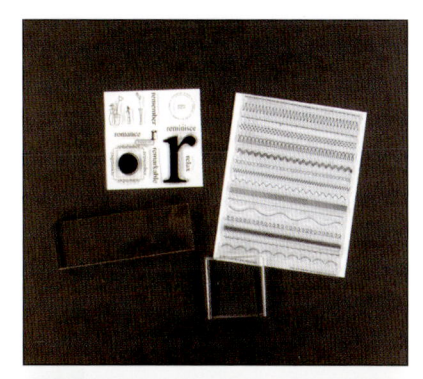

Foam-mounted stamps are usually very inexpensive in comparison to the other types of stamps. You can pick up a foam alphabet for a fraction of the cost of an acrylic or wood-mounted set. When picking out foam stamps, look for sets with a nice firm foam backing to give you plenty of stability when stamping.

Rubber, acrylic, and foam stamps fall into a few categories of styles. Letter stamps are used to stamp words one letter at a time or in combinations on long mounts. Word and phrase stamps make journaling and card making quick and simple. You can use background stamps to create your own patterned paper or background designs for additional stamping. Image stamps are all stamps that contain a picture on them.

Stamping 89

Ink Pads and Cleaners

Along with stamps, you need ink pads to begin stamping. The number of different types of stamp pads and their varying uses can make the choices staggering for a beginner. Due to the constant development of new inks, this overview of ink pad types is meant as a quick guide and not a comprehensive list.

Dye-based ink pads come in a huge variety of styles and colors. You can find both water-based and waterproof dye-based ink pads. In general, dye-based inks are good for stamping on paper. They dry quickly and are easily cleaned from your stamps.

Pigment inks are perfect for embossing as they dry more slowly than most dye-based ink pads. The ink on these pads is thicker, and when dry, it is more opaque than a dye-based image. Pigment ink is permanent and waterproof. To set pigment ink on a glossy surface, you must heat emboss it.

Chalk inks share properties of pigment inks but have a much softer, chalk-like quality to the stamped images. They can be used for embossing, and they are also beautiful when using direct-to-paper inking techniques.

Specialty ink pads include embossing inks, watermark inks, and even glue pads. Embossing ink pads are clear or slightly tinted and are used for heat embossing with colored powders. Watermark pads bring out a subtle image from the color of the background paper. Glue pads are used to stamp an image in glue so that it can be sprinkled with glitter, micro beads, or flocking.

The easiest way to clean a stamp is with an alcohol-free baby wipe. Spray cleaners with fuzzy pads for wiping off the ink and drying the stamps also work very well. Due to the variety of stamps and inks available, it is good to read the manufacturer's directions when using stamp cleaners.

Stamping 91

Stamping Lettering

Letter stamps are fabulous for scrapbook page titles, art journaling, and card making. A couple of simple tips and tricks will take the frustration out of trying to achieve perfectly aligned stamped letters.

Letter stamps come in a huge variety of fonts and sizes. To begin, select a style and size that matches the theme of your project and the space that is available for the stamped word.

1. Select an inkpad that is permanent, acid-free, and fade-resistant in a color that coordinates with the project. Press a stamp letter on the stamp pad firmly. Tap it on the pad a couple of times to be sure the whole image is inked.

② Press the inked stamp on the paper where desired. Continue with the rest of the letters in the title. Allow to dry completely before you add photos or embellishments.

③ Lining up the letters can be a challenge when stamping one letter at a time. One technique is to tilt or raise and lower each letter slightly, making the title fun and funky.

Another way to line up lettering is to stamp the letters with plenty of space in between each one on a separate piece of cardstock. Then cut or punch out shapes such as rectangles or circles around each letter. This makes it easy to line up the letters on a piece of matting cardstock.

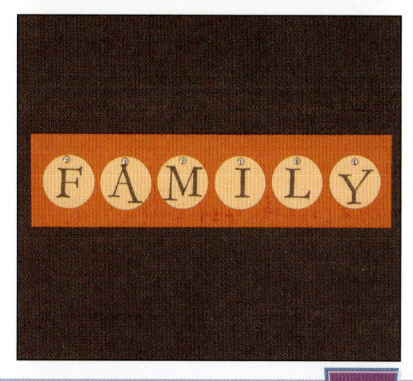

Stamping 93

Stamping with Bleach

Some colored cardstock allows you to lighten the color with bleach. Before using this technique, experiment with your paper of choice to see how it responds to a dab of bleach. If the color lightens nicely, you know that you have a winner. This process should be completed in a well-ventilated area.

---

1 Select paper that you have pre-tested and that has responded well to the bleaching process. Place a folded piece of paper towel on a plate and wet it with bleach, just until the whole towel is damp. This becomes your stamp pad. Press a rubber or foam stamp letter into the paper towel lightly, making sure the entire letter comes in contact with the bleach.

2 Press the wet stamp on the paper where desired. Continue with the rest of the letters in the title.

Note: You should wash off your stamps after stamping with bleach; simply rinse them with clean water and let dry.

The bleached title words are the perfect accent for this beach-themed scrapbook page. Always be sure to let the bleach dry completely before adding photos to the page.

Stamping 95

Pieced Stamping

Combining stamps to create an overall design is a popular technique in stamping. Many stamp sets are designed with this in mind.

1. Decide what you would like the finished image to look like. This example uses the flower stem, flower, and center circle.

2. On a piece of creamy white cardstock, stamp each of the images in different colors.

3. Carefully cut out each piece. After cutting out the stem, direct-to-paper inking is added to solidify the color.

④ Tie a small piece of ribbon around the stem and adhere it to the card.

⑤ Use double-sided foam adhesive squares to affix the flower to the top of the stem. The foam causes the flower to pop off the card.

⑥ Add the center to the middle of the flower to complete the card.

Stamping 97

Double Stamping

Stamping one image on top of another is called *double stamping*. When you double stamp using the same ink color, you achieve a beautiful and subtle tone-on-tone effect. This look is perfect for heritage scrapbooking, collage art, and creating cards with an old-world look.

① Select a background stamp that creates solid coverage. The stamp used here is a rustic square.

② Stamp another image onto the square using the same color ink. The image shown here is a travel-themed collage.

③ Using a tag punch turned upside down so that you can see where you are punching, create a mini-tag.

④ Use a dark-brown ink pad to ink the edges of the tags to complete the aged, travel-worn look.

The completed card is perfect for an anniversary card. The outside of the card reads, "Remember When . . ." while the inside says, "We met. We kissed. We fell in love. I love you even more today."

Heat Embossing

Formal invitations and fancy cards are printed with raised, embossed ink for added elegance. You can create this same look on your stamped images using embossing powder and a heat gun.

1 You need a stamp, a pigment ink pad (an embossing ink pad, or VersaMark ink pad will also work), embossing powder, a heat gun, and a tray or piece of cardstock to catch the extra powder.

2 Ink the stamp and press the image onto cardstock. For heat embossing, you need an ink that dries relatively slowly, which is why a dye-based ink pad does not work for this project.

Paper Crafts VISUAL Quick Tips

③ Immediately, while the ink is still wet, generously sprinkle the embossing powder over the image and tap or shake to remove excess powder.

④ Use a heat gun (not a hair dryer; heat guns are much hotter) to melt the embossing power. Hold the gun about 6" away from the paper and watch for the color change to know when the powder has finished melting.

⑤ For this completed card, cut out the embossed flowers and attach them to the card with a brad. Clear glitter embossing powder is used here, and so the finish is shiny with a touch of sparkle.

Stamping

Embellishing Stamping

Stamped projects are taken to the next level of creativity by adding color, sparkle, and texture. This project is a beautiful framed piece of artwork for a baby's nursery. It would make a fabulous gift, or you could use the same steps and supplies to make a greeting card.

1. To begin, stamp an image of a bunny floating with a balloon onto a piece of white cardstock using a pigment-based black ink pad.

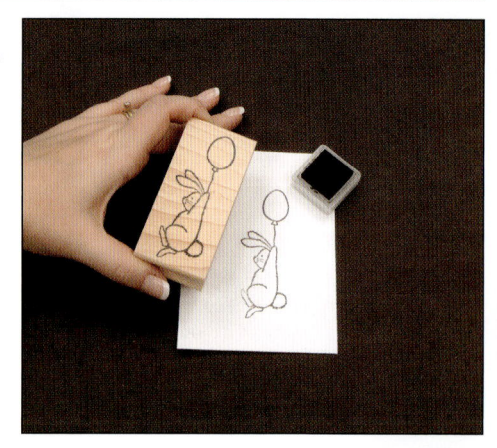

2. While the ink is still wet, sprinkle the image with glitter embossing powder. Use a heat gun to melt the powder; it is complete when the whole image is shiny and slightly sparkly.

3. Use a brush tip marker to color the balloon. You can use a permanent, acid-free marker, or a watercolor marker for this project.

4. Use chalk to add brown color to the bunny with bits of pink chalk around his tummy and on his cheek. Use blue to color the sky, leaving some white showing to look like fluffy clouds.

5. Tie a small piece of ribbon in a knot and adhere it to the string of the balloon with a GlueDot.

6. Use a glitter gel to add some sparkle to the balloon.

   Note: You could also use a liquid glue and powder glitter, but that will give you a solid mass of glitter that doesn't allow the color of the balloon to show through as well as the gel does.

CONTINUED ON NEXT PAGE

Stamping 103

Embellishing
Stamping *(continued)*

7 Add liquid appliqué to the bunny's tail and allow it to dry for at least 2 to 3 hours; overnight is preferable.

8 Use a heat gun to set the liquid appliqué, causing it to puff up, making a fluffy bunny tail.

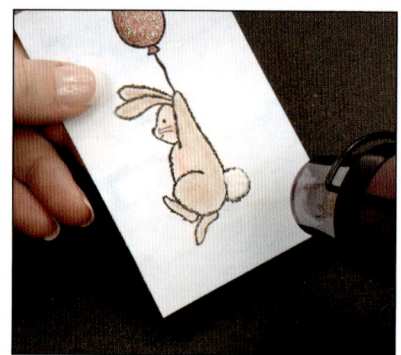

9 Using a piece of white cardstock as a base, assemble the background for the stamped piece using patterned papers.

10 Add a touch of glitter gel to the design on the papers.

11 Trim down the stamped image and double-mat it.

12 Mount it to the background with foam tape for extra dimension.

The completed design is framed in a beautiful white wood frame. A pink ribbon has been added as a hanger.

chapter 6

Crafting Techniques

Paper crafting can be as simple as combining pieces of solid cardstock to create a greeting card, or as complex as inking, chalking, folding, embellishing, and combining papers to create a work of art. A few easy techniques can help you turn even the simplest paper craft into an expression of your creativity.

Texture on Paper	**108**
Inking	**110**
Chalking	**111**
Geometric Borders	**112**
Serendipity Squares	**114**
Paper Piecing	**116**
Sewing on Paper	**120**
Folded Paper Ribbon	**122**
Vellum Envelope	**124**
Quilling	**126**
Quilling Combined Shapes	**129**
Quilling a Bouquet of Roses	**130**
Eyelets	**132**
Brads	**134**
Silk Flowers	**136**

Texture on Paper

Paper tearing is quicker and adds more texture than cutting paper with a trimmer or scissors. Tearing requires no special tools; however, a few pointers will help you get your paper tearing just right. Sanding, crumpling, and ironing are some other simple techniques that add texture to paper crafting projects.

TEARING

Hold the part of the cardstock that you want to keep in your left hand. Slowly tear the paper toward you, using your right hand to pull while your left hand gives stability to the paper and your thumbs help guide the tear.

On this scrapbook page, the entire background is made up of layered, torn papers. Cardstock or patterned paper with a white core shows as a white fuzzy edge when torn. This white edge can be chalked, inked, or used as is in your design.

SANDING

Cardstock and patterned paper with a white core undergo a dramatic transformation when sanded lightly with a piece of sandpaper. The white shows through the colored layer, making the paper look aged and weathered.

CRUMPLING

Cardstock has a fabulous textured surface when crumpled and then flattened back out. To make crumpling both easier and more effective, spray the surface with a light mist of water first. When the paper is damp, crumpling creates a rough texture throughout the surface.

IRONING

Take crumpling up a notch by ironing the crumpled cardstock. Ironing helps the paper dry quickly and seals in the creases for a leather-like appearance. Set the iron on "cotton" and keep it moving around while pressing the paper to avoid scorching.

Crafting Techniques

Inking

Ink pads are not just for rubber stamping. You can also use them to add color and texture to paper for cards, scrapbooking, collage, and other paper crafts.

DIRECT TO PAPER

To accent the edges of cardstock as shown on this tag, hold the ink pad perpendicular to the edge of the paper and lightly brush the pad down its length. Continue brushing the pad along the edge of the paper all the way around each piece you want to highlight.

RUB ON INK

Age your papers or cardstocks by rubbing ink into the paper to give it a "tea stain" or old-world look. Simply dab a makeup sponge onto the ink pad and then rub the sponge over the paper. Start light and add more layers of ink until you have the desired shade.

Chalking

Chalks come in a variety of packaging and sizes. You can get them in individual squares, pie-shaped triangles, or even in pencils.

Chalk adheres best to paper when it has some texture to grab onto. It is perfect for highlighting a torn cardstock edge.

Chalk is ideal for highlighting words in a paragraph of journaling. Outline select words with a fine-tip pen, and lightly chalk.

Chalks are perfect for use with stencils. To create your own stencil, you can chalk around die-cut letters and then remove them to leave a chalk shadow.

Crafting Techniques

Geometric Borders

Paper punched into basic geometric shapes can have a huge impact on the overall design of your projects. The shapes can be arranged in a border stripe or divided up to fill in blank space.

Use punches to make shapes in coordinating colors to go with your card or scrapbook page. Choose one color and shape as the background for each design. In this example, the background is a square.

Layer the shapes as desired to decorate the squares. Allow some of the shapes to extend off the edges of the bottom shapes. Use scissors to trim the shape even with the edge of the base.

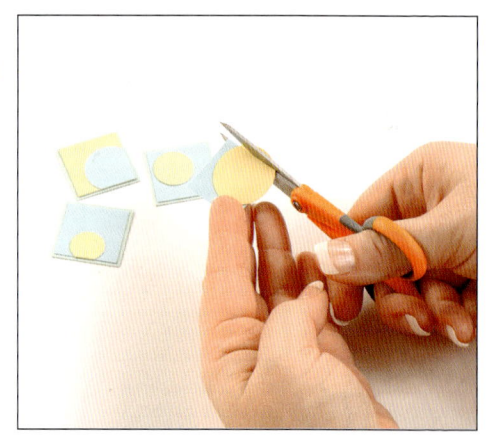

Mat each finished square and add an embellishment such as an eyelet or brad to complete the shape. These finished squares can be added to your layout in a line to create a border.

You can also use the decorated squares to add interest in open spaces of your layout. On this page, squares are used to accent the photo and fill space on the left side of the page.

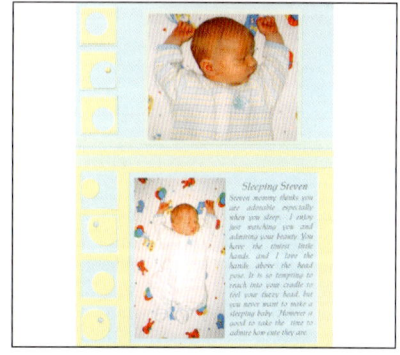

Geometric borders and squares can also be used on greeting cards. The technique is simple and the clean lines add interest to any crafting project.

Crafting Techniques 113

Serendipity Squares

Serendipity means "happy accident." Mix up your scraps of paper and you will be pleasantly surprised with beautiful serendipity squares that you can use to decorate greeting cards, mini-books, and scrapbook pages.

1 Start with a large sheet of cardstock—6" x 6" is large enough. Begin layering torn pieces of cardstock onto this background sheet. Make sure that each piece you add is completely glued down to the background sheet.

2 Further embellish the background sheet by adding rubber stamping. Simply stamp a design in a random pattern all over the piece. Be sure to turn the stamp and also stamp over the edge occasionally.

❸ When you are happy with the coverage of the background cardstock, use your trimmer to cut it into squares. These squares can be any size you want—1½" is a good choice for your first project. Mat each of the squares on a coordinating color of cardstock.

❹ Add the squares to your layout. You can place them in a row to form a border or scatter them over the page to fill in blank spaces. They look best in groupings of two or three squares each.

On this scrapbook page, the serendipity squares are made up of textured papers, punches, and die-cuts. The texture of the squares accents the texture of the subject of the photos.

Crafting Techniques 115

Paper Piecing

Paper piecing is the art of creating pictures with paper. Each piece is cut out and layered to make the finished project. Although the process can be time-consuming, the finished look can make a paper-craft project extra special.

1. To transfer the pattern from p. 208 to your choice of colored cardstock, begin by laying a piece of tracing paper or vellum over the top of the pattern, and trace. If the pattern has a lot of pieces, you may want to label each one as you trace it.

2. Flip the tracing paper over and use a small amount of adhesive to attach the traced pattern to the cardstock. By turning the piece over before you attach it, any damage done by the glue is on the back of the finished cardstock piece. Now cut out each piece.

Paper Crafts VISUAL Quick Tips

❸ In this pattern, the giraffe's mane has some special instructions. First transfer the pattern and cut out the cardstock into the long rectangle of the mane.

❹ Next, cut three-quarters of the way through the paper over and over again, as close together as possible—leaving a scant 1/8" strip between each cut. Continue down the entire rectangle.

❺ Once all the lines have been cut, start again at the beginning of the strip and snip out every other piece. This leaves the rectangle looking like a comb, or a giraffe's mane.

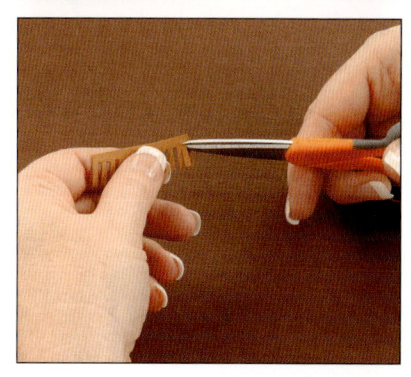

CONTINUED ON NEXT PAGE

Crafting Techniques

Paper Piecing
(continued)

6 Put the pieces together as shown in the finished example. Adhere them to matted rectangles that coordinate with the scrapbook page and use a black fine-tip journaling pen to outline each piece. You can also use this pen to add features to each animal.

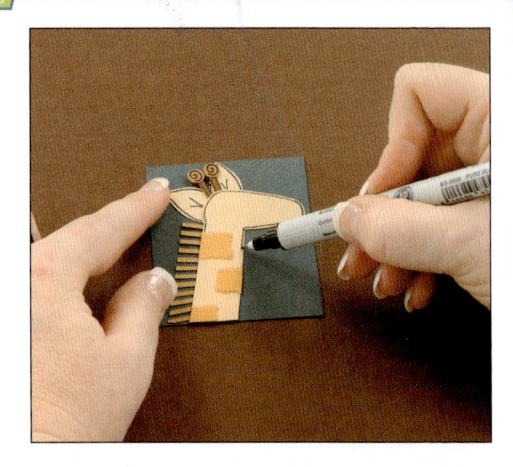

7 Complete the piece with a touch of chalk. Use a cotton swab to add pink chalk to the inside of the giraffe's ears and the cheek.

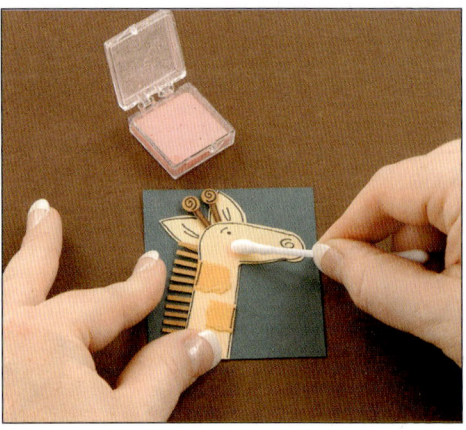

8 Follow the same basic steps to complete the tiger and the monkey. The tiger's stripes are added with a black fine-tip pen. If desired, outline each animal's rectangle with dashes and dots.

The pattern used here can also be used to create adorable birthday party invitations. This pattern is also used in Chapter 9 to create home décor.

TIP

You can make your own paper piecing patterns using shapes from children's coloring books or from clip art. You can also find dozens of free patterns online at http://scrapbooking.about.com.

Crafting Techniques 119

Sewing on Paper

It's true! You can use your sewing machine to stitch on paper. This easy technique can be used to create beautiful scrapbook pages and textured paper-craft projects.

① Trim cardstock or paper pieces as desired and tack them down on your layout with small bits of adhesive. Set the stitch length on your sewing machine to a long setting so that the holes will be farther apart as you stitch through the paper.

② Choose either a straight or zigzag stitch and carefully sew along your paper. Do not back up over the same spot to tie off the end or you may tear the paper. Finish by trimming off the threads.

In this layout, the top and bottom borders are stitched to the page. This step takes just minutes to complete and gives the page a finished feel. The flower embellishments on this page, purchased from the sewing section at a craft store, complement the sewing.

Folded Paper Ribbon

Paper can be folded and sewn onto cardstock to give the texture and illusion of ribbon. The steps are simple, yet the finished project is sure to impress.

1. Cut and score cardstock to create a greeting card base. Also cut a strip of patterned paper that is 1½" wide.

2. Fold the patterned paper strip at ¾" and ¼" over and over, all the way down the strip. To hold the folds in place, add a strip of photo tape down the back of the folded strip.

❸ Use the photo tape on the back of the folded strip to adhere it to the card. Stitch using your sewing machine down the length of the folded strip. The example shown here is stitched twice, once near the top and once near the bottom of the strip.

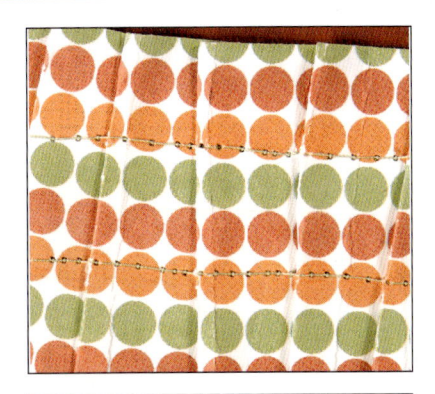

❹ The finished card is simple, but fun. By simply switching out the colors and prints of the paper, this technique can be used to create cards for any theme.

Folded paper ribbons can also be used to embellish scrapbook pages. The layout shown here uses three different strips of folded and stitched patterned papers.

Crafting Techniques 123

Vellum Envelope

A vellum envelope is the perfect place to store memorabilia on a scrapbook page, or tuck away a gift card on a greeting card. The vellum protects the contents while allowing you to see through it to know what's inside.

1. Copy and resize the pattern for the vellum envelope on p. 209. Trace the pattern for the envelope onto the vellum.

2. Cut out the envelope and crease on the fold lines.

❸ Use a large circle punch to create a notch in the front of the pocket. Turn the circle punch upside down so you can see exactly where you are punching.

❹ Fold and glue down the tabs to finish the envelope. Be sure to glue the flaps to the back of the envelope and not inside of it; that way, they won't catch every time you insert items into the pocket.

❺ The finished pocket envelope can be attached to a scrapbook page or greeting card. You can see in this example that the envelope is the perfect size for a pair of tickets.

Crafting Techniques 125

Quilling

Quilling is one of the oldest paper crafts. It is rumored to have begun centuries ago by nuns using pieces of gilded paper edges to create elaborate works of art by wrapping the papers around a feather's quill. Today, pre-cut quilling strips and slotted tools make the craft accessible to anyone.

1. To begin quilling, you need the following supplies: a slotted quilling tool, strips of paper, liquid glue, and toothpicks. You may want to pick up a quilling board to help you make shapes of uniform size.

2. To roll the strips, begin by placing the very end of a quilling strip into the slotted end of the tool, and turn the tool to roll.

③ Once a strip is rolled, slide it off of the slotted tool and use a small amount of liquid glue on a toothpick to glue down the end. Hold the end in place for a few seconds until the glue holds.

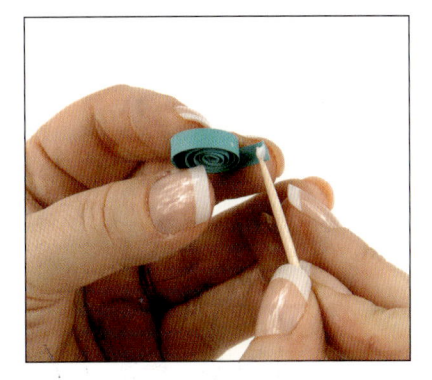

④ To adhere shapes to a greeting card or project, simply apply more liquid glue on the back of the shape with a toothpick and hold it in place for a few seconds.

You can glue shapes to one another to create simple designs. To make this heart, use a toothpick to place glue on the side of one teardrop and press it to another. Hold them together until the glue is tacky enough to hold. For more on combining shapes, see p. 129.

Crafting Techniques

Quilling
(continued)

The fundamentals of quilling are based on a collection of basic shapes. Practice making a few of each of the shapes shown below, and you will be ready to make much more intricate designs.

Quilling Basic Shapes

Tight Coil	Loose Coil	Tear Drop
Marquis	Heart	Loose Scroll
S Scroll	V Scroll	C Scroll

Quilling Combined Shapes

Once you have mastered the basic shapes in quilling, you can begin combining them to make simple designs. The ones shown here are just a few examples of the many things you can make for your cards and paper-crafting projects.

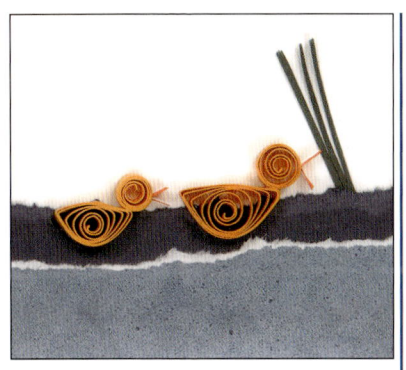

This springtime duck family is made from a form of a marquis shape and a loose circle.

Beautiful summertime flowers can be made simply from teardrop shapes with a tight circle in the center.

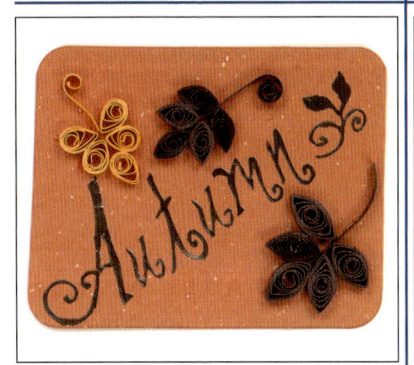

Fall leaves are made with five marquis shapes held together on a loose scroll.

A snowman can simply be made from three loose circles. Pinch a black circle into a square shape for a top hat.

Crafting Techniques

Quilling a Bouquet of Roses

① The roses are constructed on a circle punch base. Each petal is another circle punch. The center is a loose circle.

② To construct the rose, pinch the pink punched circles to give them some dimension. Glue them to the base, and add the loose circle to the center.

③ The tiny white flowers are quilled heart shapes that are glued onto the front edge of a green quilling strip.

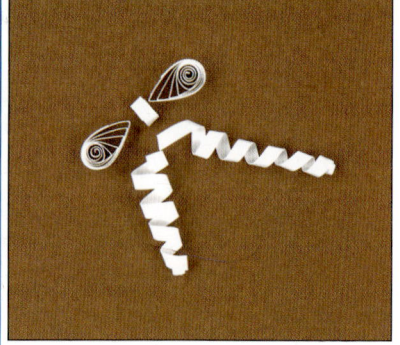

④ The bow is two teardrops, a flattened, small loose circle (for the center), and two tight circles that have been pulled open from the center to make swirly ribbons.

The completed bouquet would be gorgeous as a framed piece of artwork. Here it is shown on a "Get Well" card, but it would be equally at home on a Mother's Day, anniversary, or birthday card.

Crafting Techniques

Eyelets

Eyelets are tiny grommets. They come in a wide variety of shapes and colors, but the one thing they all have in common is that you need tools to "set" them.

1. The basic tools you need to set an eyelet include a hammer, an "anywhere" hole punch, a setter, and a mat to protect your work surface.

2. Use an "anywhere" hole punch to punch a hole the size of the shank of your eyelet in the cardstock. Place a cutting mat under the cardstock and hold the punching tool in place where you want to make the hole.

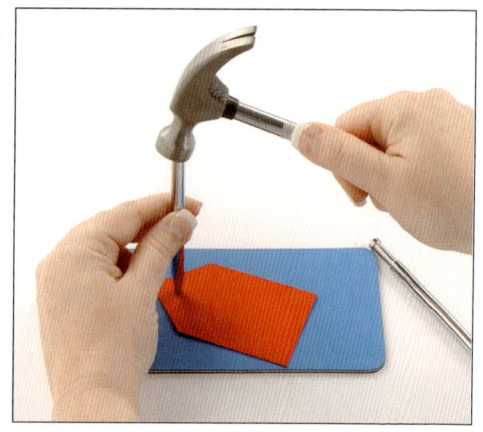

❸ Strike the top of the tool once or twice to punch a hole through the cardstock.

❹ Insert your eyelet through the hole and hold it carefully in place as you turn the cardstock over.

❺ Switch to an eyelet-setting tool. Place this tool with the tip balanced in the center of the back of the eyelet, and hit it with a hammer twice. This rolls or splits the back of the eyelet to lock it in place.

Crafting Techniques 133

Brads

Brads are extremely popular in paper crafting partly because they are very easy to use. The variety of colors and styles means that you will be able to find brads to match any project.

As you can see from this sampling, brads come in a huge variety of colors, sizes, and shapes.

① The only tools you need to set a brad are a regular office pushpin and an upside-down mouse pad.

134 **Paper Crafts VISUAL Quick Tips**

② Place your project on top of the upside-down mouse pad. Use the pushpin to poke a hole exactly where you want to place the brad. The mouse pad provides a surface that supports the paper while allowing the pin to penetrate.

③ Press the prongs of the brad through the hole. The hole made by the pushpin is perfect for mini-brads. If the brad prongs are larger than the hole, you may need to poke another one right next to it to enlarge the hole.

④ To finish setting the brad, you simply open the two prongs on the back of the project to hold the brad in place.

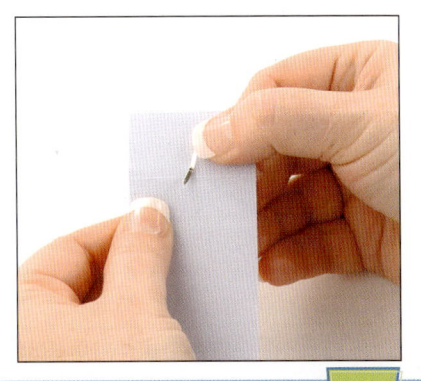

Crafting Techniques

Silk Flowers

Silk flowers are lightweight, soft, and come in beautiful colors, making them perfect decorations for paper crafting. You can add silk flowers to scrapbook pages, art journals, greeting cards, gift tags, and home décor paper crafts.

1. Start by removing the flower from the plastic stem.
2. Select a round or decorative brad that will work nicely as the center of the flower.
3. Layer two or more flowers on top of one another and position them on a cardstock square.
4. Use a pushpin to poke a hole in the middle of the flowers through the cardstock and add the brad to the center to hold the flowers in place.

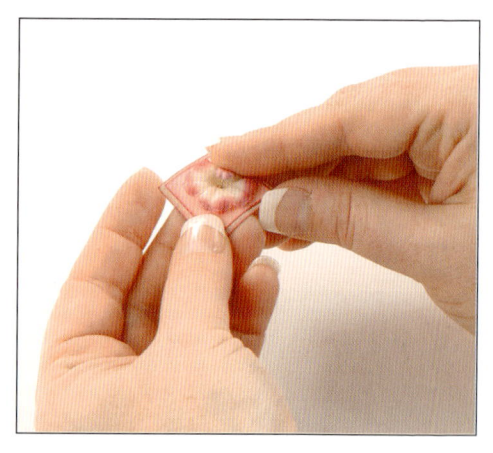

Paper Crafts VISUAL Quick Tips

Once you have completed several silk flower squares, you can add them to your scrapbook page, greeting card, or tag. The flowers add a three-dimensional touch of femininity while adding lovely texture and color. On the scrapbook page shown here, the pink flower squares accent the pretty-in-pink baby doll photos.

Crafting Techniques

chapter 7

Lettering Styles

Liven up the text on all of your paper-craft projects by trying out a new lettering style or technique. Whether you experiment with printing on vellum, ribbon, or die-cuts, or you try out clay letters or stencil paste, you will enjoy the creativity of playing with lettering styles.

Printing on Vellum 140

Printing on Transparencies 142

Printing on Cork, Fabric, and Ribbon 144

Printing on Tags and Die-Cuts 146

Label Maker Lettering 148

Stamping and Templates 150

Layered Letters 152

Shaker Letters 154

Tag Shaker Titles 156

Chipboard Monogram Letters 158

Clay Letters 162

Stencil Paste Letters 164

Printing on Vellum

Vellum allows the color of the paper or photos to show through behind your text, creating a soft, muted effect. Using your computer to print titles and text on vellum will give your greeting cards and scrapbook pages a custom-finished look.

---

1. Print your journaling on a simple, plain vellum sheet. Usually the less expensive vellum works better in an inkjet printer. Some higher-priced or printed vellum has a special coating that keeps the ink from drying smoothly. Allow the ink to dry completely before you touch the piece.

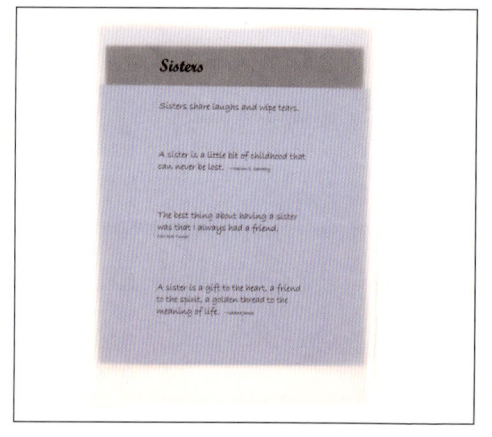

2. Trim around the printed text and attach the vellum to your photo mat or greeting card using brads or eyelets, as shown in Chapter 6.

The scrapbook page shown here has both the title and journaling printed on vellum. The vellum has been stitched to a piece of patterned paper to create window boxes that are filled with confetti snowflakes. The scrapbook page layout was designed by Jenna Tomalka.

Lettering Styles

Printing on Transparencies

Transparencies are another creative way to place text on top of a photo or piece of patterned paper while allowing the colors to show through completely. This allows you to add text anywhere on your scrapbook pages and other paper-crafting projects.

① Print your quotes or journaling on transparencies specifically designed for your printer. Inkjet printer transparencies have a textured side that holds the ink in place, so be sure to place the transparency right side up in your printer.

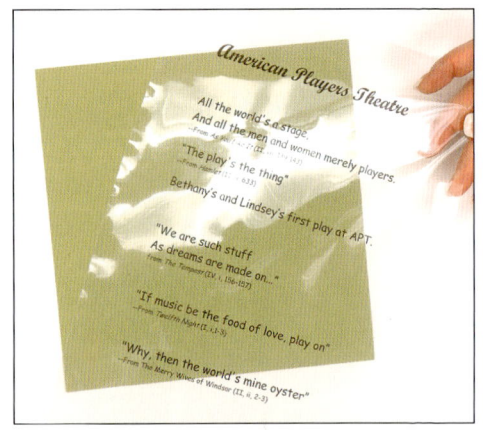

② Allow the ink to dry completely before you trim and attach the printed transparency. You can attach the transparency to your layout or card mat using brads or eyelets, as shown in Chapter 6.

142 Paper Crafts VISUAL Quick Tips

The scrapbook page shown here has both text and photos printed on transparencies. The photos have the look of a strip of film from an old movie projector with the pattern from the paper showing through them.

Lettering Styles 143

Printing on Cork, Fabric, and Ribbon

Dimensional items such as cork, fabric, and ribbon can be exciting title or card-making enhancements. Printing on these items takes a few special considerations.

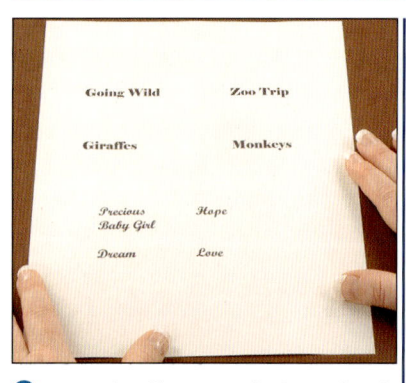

1 On regular office paper, print the words and phrases that you want to print on textured material.

2 Use a repositionable adhesive to adhere the fabric, very thin sheet cork, or ribbon over the printed words.

Note: *All printers are different. Be careful not to damage your printer by printing on materials that are too thick for it.*

3 Place the sheet back in the printer and print again; this time the printing appears on top of the textured material.

Paper Crafts VISUAL Quick Tips

This scrapbook page uses printed sheet cork. The thin cork is only slightly thicker than cardstock. Be careful running thick items through your printer to prevent jamming and damage. If you are concerned, you could achieve a similar look by rubber-stamping on the cork instead.

Lettering Styles 145

Printing on Tags and Die-Cuts

With a few simple steps, you can print on items generally considered too small to run through your printer. This simple technique allows you to print on die-cuts, tags, or in a specific spot on a piece of patterned paper.

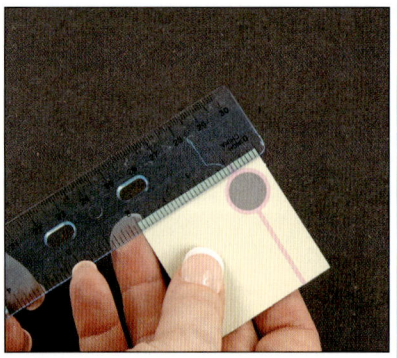

---

① To begin lining up computer printing on a die-cut or tag, measure the area you have available for text.

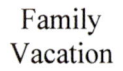

② Print text following those measurements onto a piece of regular office paper.

③ Using a light box, line up the die-cut over the text on the office paper and adhere it with temporary adhesive.

④ Place this sheet back in the printer and print again. Remove the die-cut from the office paper and add it to your card or scrapbook page.

The scrapbook page shown below used the techniques for printing on tags and die-cuts to print the title within the circles on the piece of patterned paper, and also to add journaling information to the die-cut on top of the mini-book in the lower-right corner.

Lettering Styles 147

Label Maker Lettering

Old-fashioned embossing label makers are fun text tools. You can select any color cardstock and create lettering masterpieces. The words become the embellishments on your paper-craft projects with this easy technique.

① Select cardstock that has a white core but a dark-colored surface. Cut the paper into ⅜" strips.

② Feed a strip, right side up, into an empty label maker machine. Select each letter and press the lever.

③ When you have embossed all the letters into the strip, remove the strip from the machine.

④ Use sandpaper to lightly sand the surface of the embossed letters on the strip.

The scrapbook page shown here is embellished only with words. Label maker lettering makes a striking border down the side of the page.

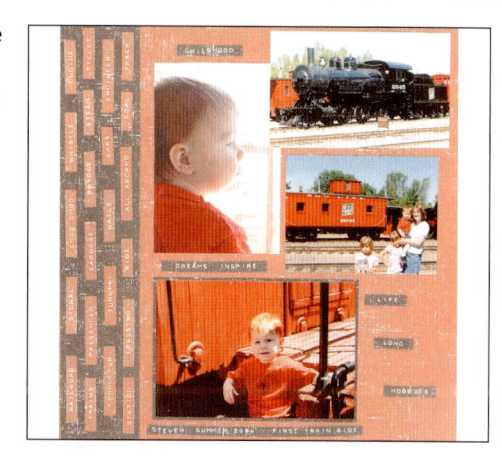

This technique can be used on any paper crafts. Here it is shown on a greeting card. The title "Happy Birthday" is created using label maker lettering.

TIP

As label makers have gained popularity in paper crafting, more fonts and styles have become available. You can now also find tapes for your label maker in a rainbow of colors.

Lettering Styles 149

Stamping and Templates

You can make unique titles for your scrapbook pages, greeting cards, and gift tags by combining lettering templates with rubber-stamped letters.

① Using a pencil, very lightly draw a straight line across the center of a strip of cardstock.

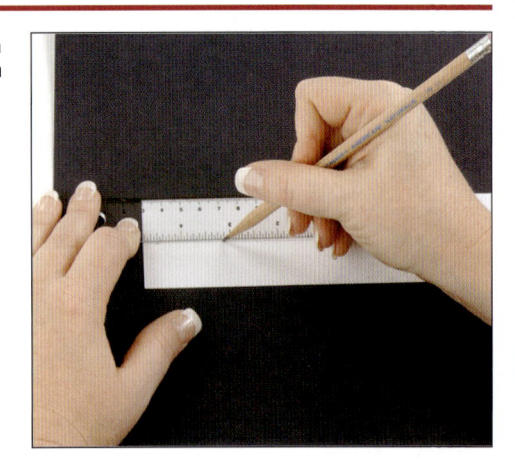

② On the line, stamp all but the last word of your title or phrase.

❸ Trace the last word of the title using a lettering template over the top of the stamped letters, being careful to stop your pen whenever it intersects with the rubber-stamped words.

❹ Erase your initial pencil line. Fill in the traced letters with colored pencils and mat on colored cardstock to complete your title.

The finished title reads "Back to School." This would work equally well for phrases like "Happy Birthday" or "Thank You Very Much."

Lettering Styles

Layered Letters

By tracing letters with templates and cutting them out of different colors of cardstock and patterned papers, you can create beautiful layered letters. The layers of paper can accent any paper-craft project by making your letters really stand out.

1. Choose coordinating colors or prints of cardstock or even patterned paper. Create a strip using these colors of paper that shows each one as much or as little as you desire, making sure they are close enough to each other that they will all appear on each letter traced from your template.

2. Make sure that the strips of paper are completely adhered together or to a base of cardstock. When you begin cutting out letters, any little parts that are not completely stuck down may fall off. Use a pencil to lightly trace each letter of your title.

③ Carefully cut out the letters and adhere them to a background of cardstock to complete your title.

Embellishments such as stickers, buttons, or ribbon may be added to finish the look. The beach title shown here is decorated with beaded stickers.

By changing the colors and patterns of the papers, you can use this technique for any theme or occasion. The title shown here would be perfect for a theme-park scrapbook page.

Lettering Styles 153

Shaker Letters

Make die-cut titles three-dimensional by creating fun shaker titles. Your paper-craft projects will come to life when the titles have movement and depth.

1. Layer papers on a strip of cardstock.
2. Die-cut the letters needed for your title from the layered strip to create letters with colored stripes. Die-cut the same letters from a coordinating color of craft foam.

3. Continue until you have cut out your entire title from both layered cardstock and craft foam.
4. Lay out your letters to double check that you have spelled the word correctly and have all the letters that you need.

5. Adhere the foam letters to a piece of cardstock or to the front of your greeting card. Select one or more letters to fill with beads.
6. Cover each foam letter that is not filled with beads with a matching layered cardstock die-cut letter.

7. Cut a small piece of plastic page protector or a piece of transparency to size so that it seals in the beads in your title letter.
8. Adhere the piece of plastic in place.

9. Once the beads are sealed in place and the glue is dry, finish the shaker letter by adding the layered cardstock die-cut letter on top.

Lettering Styles 155

Tag Shaker Titles

1. Tags turned into shakers can also be used for titles. Die-cut four tags: one from base cardstock, one from craft foam, one from a clear plastic, and one from patterned paper.

2. Take the foam tag and the patterned paper tag and die-cut a letter from your title from the center of each of them.

3. Adhere the foam to the cardstock base tag using liquid permanent glue. Fill the letter shape with seed beads, and adhere the clear plastic tag over the foam base to seal in the beads.

4. Add the final tag—patterned paper—on top of the shaker to complete the letter. Repeat these steps for each letter in the title.

The scrapbook page layout shown here uses shaker tag letters to spell out "TOYS." The letters have been strung on red ribbon to make it appear that the tags are hanging on the page.

Lettering Styles 157

Chipboard Monogram Letters

Laying chipboard (the cardboard found on the back of a pad of paper) with patterned paper allows you to create over-sized letters with dimension.

① Select a font on your computer that will create a letter that is easy to cut out. Print that letter in a large font size.

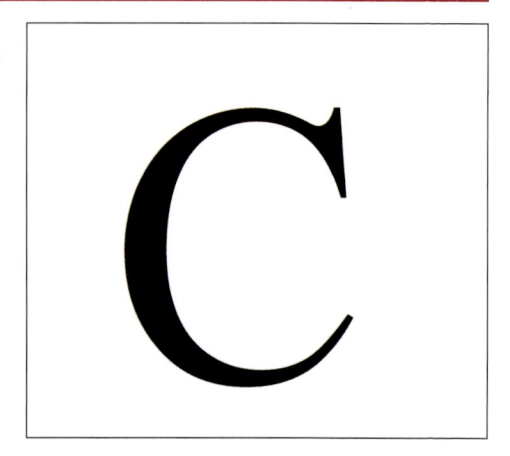

② Use removable adhesive to adhere the printed letter to a piece of chipboard.

Paper Crafts VISUAL Quick Tips

③ Carefully cut out the letter from the chipboard, trying not to bend and weaken the chipboard as you cut.

④ Permanently adhere the front side of the chipboard letter to the back of a piece of patterned paper.

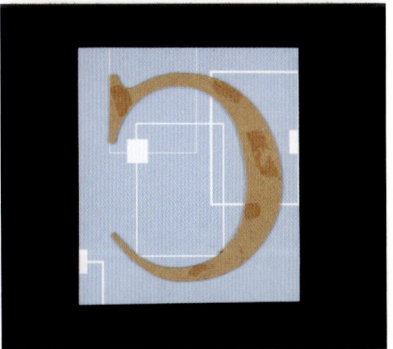

⑤ Once again cut out the letter. You can use a piece of sand paper to smooth out the edges of the covered chipboard letter when it is completely cut out.

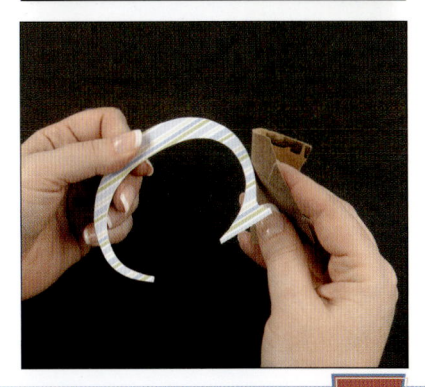

CONTINUED ON NEXT PAGE

Lettering Styles

Chipboard Monogram Letters *(continued)*

CHIPBOARD LETTER SCRAPBOOK PAGE

The large chipboard letter "C" on this scrapbook page draws attention to the title "Carefree." Chipboard letters allow you to easily make embellishments that can be coordinated to go with any theme paper craft project.

Mikhail – I love to watch you play. You have no worries, no inhibitions. Your **carefree** attitude constantly reminds me that you are our little miracle. Spring 2005

CHIPBOARD NUMBER BIRTHDAY CARD

Chipboard numbers are perfect for birthday and anniversary cards. Create several and use them to embellish birthday party invitations or graduation announcements.

Lettering Styles

Clay Letters

For years, crafters have been using polymer clay for jewelry making, sculpting, and more. Both this clay and air-dry paper clay can be used to make three-dimensional letters for scrapbook page titles.

1. To get a variegated color letter, mix two or more shades of clay together by twisting and rolling them until you have achieved the desired blend. This example mixes blue and white polymer clay.

2. Use a small rolling pin or a piece of wooden dowel to roll the clay out to an even ¼" thickness.

❸ Press cookie-cutter type letter cutters into the clay for each letter needed for the title. Bake the letters on a cookie sheet following the manufacturer's directions.

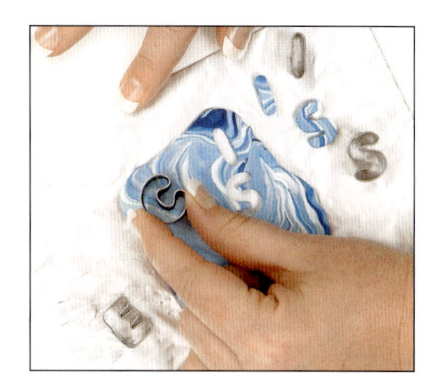

❹ Remove from the oven and let cool. Adhere the letters to your cardstock title mat with adhesive dots or liquid glue.

❺ Embellish the completed title with stickers, ribbon, or die-cuts. The title shown here has been finished off with a 3-D die-cut embellishment of a cruise ship from EK Success.

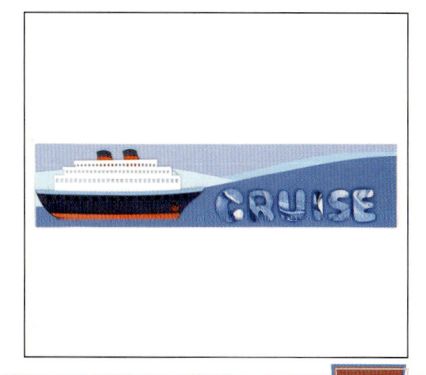

Lettering Styles 163

Stencil Paste Letters

Acid-free stencil paste makes letters that have both dimension and texture. The paste dries to an almost rubbery consistency, and so it won't break, crack, or flake off of your paper crafts.

① Select stencil paste that is acid-free and made for paper crafts. You also need a lettering stencil and a plastic putty knife.

② Mask off surrounding letters. Use the putty knife to spread an even layer of paste over the letter.

③ Carefully lift the stencil off of the background cardstock, leaving just the shape of the letter in stencil paste behind, and allow to dry.

④ Adhere the completed letter on cardstock to your scrapbook page or greeting card.

The texture of the stencil paste letter accents the architecture shown in the photos of this completed scrapbook page.

Doors of Dublin

The colors, smells, and textures of traveling in Ireland all made the experience a trip to remember. These colorful doors caught my eye.

Lettering Styles

chapter 8

Adding Artistic Flair

Paper-crafting techniques and ideas can inspire you, but it is your own artistic flair and creativity that turn a craft project into a work of art. If you are looking to take your crafting into the realm of artwork, the projects in this chapter will help you to stretch your artistic side.

Collage Wall Art **168**
Tissue Paper Decoupage **170**
Art Journaling **172**
Sample Art Journals **174**
Artist Trading Cards **176**
Artist Trading Card Gallery **178**

Collage Wall Art

Collage began as a novelty art form in the early twentieth century when artists such as Picasso began adding dimension to their works by adding metal, wood, and paper to traditional art canvases. Collage simply means to create something by assembling a variety of different media. Using a canvas to create a simple combination of papers and embellishments is an easy way to give collage a try.

1. To begin, select a canvas or chipboard background and cover it with paper to create your background. A simple white background allows the art to "pop" toward the center of the canvas.

2. To complete your piece, you need to decide on papers and embellishments that will work together to create a design or image. Homemade, textured, and patterned papers may be combined with ribbon, buttons, metal embellishments, fibers, wood, and even feathers.

The canvas shown here uses layered papers, leaves cut from sheer fabric, metal leaf charms, and ribbon to give the piece texture and dimension.

Adding Artistic Flair

Tissue Paper Decoupage

Decoupage is a form of collage art. It simply entails gluing papers or pictures in layers onto an object, with several layers of glue or decoupage medium to protect it. A simple project to exercise your collage and decoupage creativity is a tissue paper "painting."

1 You need a variety of colors of tissue paper, white liquid glue, a foam brush, and a canvas board. You can find canvas boards in a variety of sizes at your local craft store.

2 To begin, pour several tablespoons of white glue into a disposable dish and mix in water to thin the glue out slightly. A mixture of 1 part water to 3 parts glue will work.

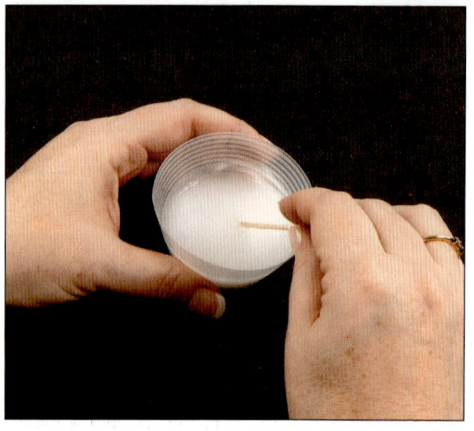

③ Tear the tissue paper into strips or chunks. You may want to tear some pieces into shapes that will form your picture.

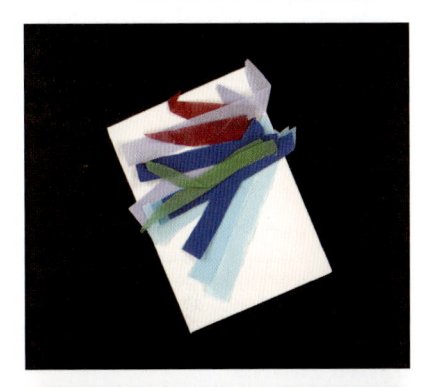

④ Brush glue thinly on a portion of the canvas and add tissue paper. Add more glue over the top of the tissue paper to help secure it in place and protect it. Continue adding layers, alternating between glue and tissue paper.

⑤ The project shown here uses a combination of torn and cut tissue paper. The wings of the dragonfly are made from silver metallic tissue paper. As a final touch, letters forming the word "DREAM" are stamped on a sheet of tissue paper and added to the picture.

Adding Artistic Flair 171

Art Journaling

An art journal combines personal introspection with artistic creativity. Most art journals are meant to be seen only by the creator; therefore, anything goes. You don't have to be an expert at painting, stamping, drawing, or collage—you just get to let go and have fun experimenting. Helen South, the Drawing/Sketching Guide for About.com, says, "It is good to think of your art journal as a private diary, a place to explore freely."

For Helen, " . . . art journaling is about using collage elements and found images with or without text, as a form of diary entry. It might simply record the day's events or respond to them in some way. . . . The journal page can be as informal as a rough collage of magazine images or a carefully worked and layered creation using exotic papers and gold leaf." Some simple things to keep in mind while working in your art journal are listed here and on the next page.

USING FOUND IMAGES

Select images that express your mood, thoughts, or feelings. You could use clip art, magazine cut-outs, stamped images, or photos. The mood of the images will help you decide on the colors and embellishments for your piece.

Paper Crafts VISUAL Quick Tips

ADDING COLOR

Add color to your journal entry with papers, painting, colored pencils, chalks, or direct-to-paper inking techniques. The colors should support or reflect the mood of the piece.

ADDING TEXT

The text for your art journal entries can be as simple as handwritten journaling, or your thoughts might be better expressed by rub-on phrases, cut-out magazine text, stamped words, or quote stickers.

EMBELLISHING

Flat items are best in your journal to keep it from becoming too bulky. Some good choices include rubber stamping, fibers and ribbons, rub-on's, stickers, or pressed flowers.

Adding Artistic Flair | 173

Sample Art Journals

Art journal entries can be used to experiment with a specific artistic style, or to express feelings, thoughts, or ideas. Helen South found these images on a royalty-free photo site, and thought that the man and woman seem to have a story behind them. She expressed that story in her journal entry with color, text, and additional images.

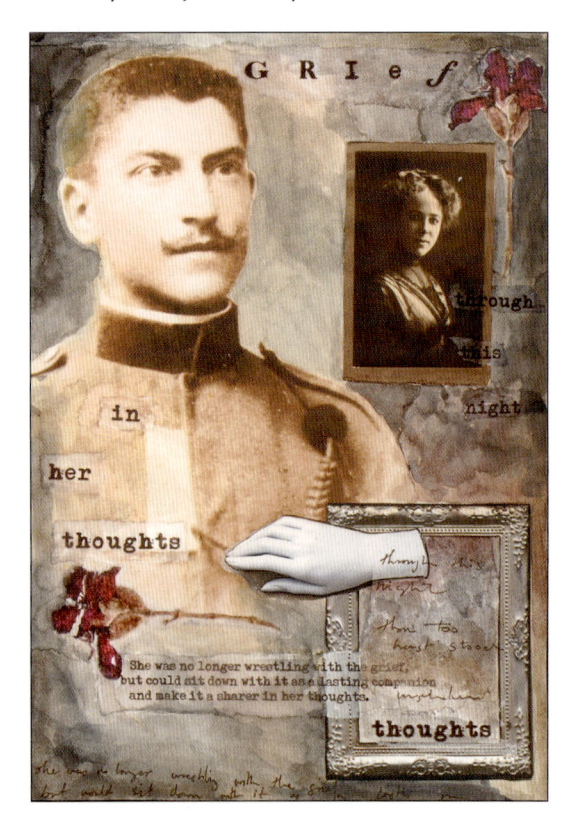

Art journaling is about expressing your thoughts and feelings on paper. If you have a background in scrapbooking, you may feel more comfortable starting with pages like those shown here. The images on the pages are photos that have been printed on white cardstock. The photos were inked, mounted on patterned paper, and then dry-brushed with acrylic paints.

Adding Artistic Flair | 175

Artist Trading Cards

Artist trading cards are pieces of art in miniature. These tiny artistic expressions are meant to be traded with others. Swaps and trading communities abound on the Internet.

Artist trading cards (ATCs) have a standard size of 2½" x 3½". This is approximately the size of a standard playing card.

The base is usually cardstock or thin chipboard. Other creative materials include leather, metal, stiffened fabric, or wood. You can start with a piece of base cardstock (or a playing card) cut to size, or work on a larger sheet and cut it down as the final step.

ATCs are usually handmade, although digital ATCs are gaining popularity. They may be rubber stamped, embossed, stitched, collaged, or painted. Pretty much anything goes. Some people restrict the thickness, or lumpiness, of their embellishments so that the cards can be stored in baseball card-style sleeves.

An ATC can be an individual work of art, or if you create several that are the same or similar, they are called an edition, which is numbered on the back of the card (for example, 1/8, 2/8, and so on). If you create several cards of a related theme, then you have made a series.

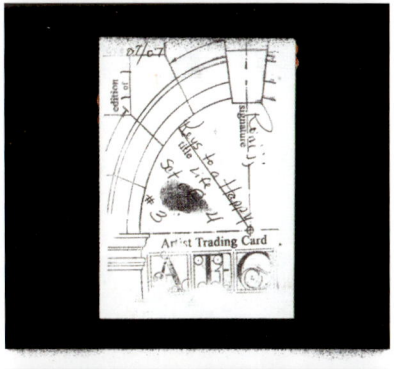

The artist should sign the back of each card. Some people include additional information, such as naming their creation, the date that it was created, and contact information. Rubber stamps are a quick and decorative way to label the back of your ATCs.

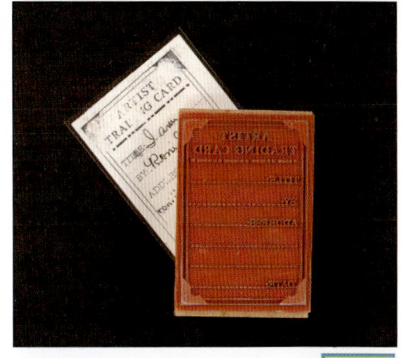

Adding Artistic Flair

Artist Trading Card Gallery

The cards shown on these two pages were created by Veronica Johnson. She used a variety of techniques and embellishments. Notice how she added dimension without a lot of bulk to her cards by attaching elements with foam tape.

The four artist trading cards shown here are a series that Veronica titled "Keys to a Happy Life." They are embellished with old keys and glass slides. The slides have been wrapped in foil tape to finish off the edges.

Adding Artistic Flair 179

chapter 9

Crafting Home Décor

The techniques used in paper crafts such as scrapbooking, rubber stamping, and card making can also be used to create unique home décor and special gifts for family and friends. The projects in this chapter can be hung on a wall, displayed on a desk, or even draped around a banister.

Wooden Photo Cubes **182**
Photo Cube Puzzle **184**
Decorated Photo Frames **186**
Paper Pieced and Decoupaged Lamp **188**
Scrapbooking on Canvas **190**
Sparkle Lights **192**
Tween Mobile **194**
Art Clock **196**
Letter Blocks **198**

Wooden Photo Cubes

Photo cubes are an innovative way to display your family photos on a shelf or fireplace mantel. Made from simple wooden cubes, these blocks are easy and fun to make. After you make a set for yourself, you will want to make several to give as gifts.

① Purchase or cut 2 to 3" wooden cubes.

② Paint the cubes with acrylic paint and let them dry completely. Watered-down paint allows the grain of the wood to show.

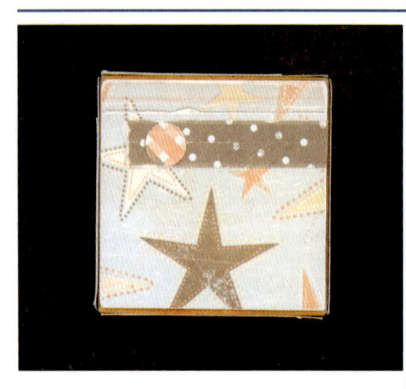

③ Add pieces of patterned paper to several sides of the cubes.

④ Add photos and embellishments to complete the cubes.

Paper Crafts VISUAL Quick Tips

This set of completed cubes is pulled together by using coordinating colors of paint and a set of patterned papers and embellishments. The sides display treasured family photos.

Crafting Home Décor 183

Photo Cube Puzzle

When you put four photo cubes together to create a square, you can turn the whole thing into a photo puzzle. Each side of the blocks, when put together correctly, displays one of six "miniature scrapbook pages."

1 To begin, you need four identical square blocks.

2 Measure the size of the four blocks together and create mini-scrapbook page squares to fit on the blocks.

3 Cut each scrapbook page into four pieces and attach them to the cubes with photo tape.

4 Turn the cubes and add another page, continuing until all six sides are covered.

Paper Crafts VISUAL Quick Tips

Display the photo cube puzzle on a piece of mat board that you have covered with adhesive-backed felt. The felt keeps the face-down photos from getting scratched.

Crafting Home Décor | 185

Decorated Photo Frames

Possibly one of the simplest home décor paper-craft projects is a decorated photo frame. You can purchase a frame at your local craft store or look for one that is sold in a kit with trim and embellishments, such as this one from Making Memories.

① To begin, paint the frame or cover it with patterned paper. You may choose to sand the edges or surface of the frame to give it a rough, weathered appearance.

② Add embellishments. You can use a hot glue gun or tacky glue to adhere ribbons, trims, flowers, and buttons to the frame.

Paper Crafts VISUAL Quick Tips

The completed photo frame adds a personal touch to the display of any photo. This simple project makes a fabulous gift for bridal showers, graduations, baby showers, and weddings.

Crafting Home Décor

Paper Pieced and Decoupaged Lamp

Combine paper piecing and decoupage techniques to create adorable home décor. This lamp project would be perfect for display on a dresser in a child's room.

---

① Start by covering a plain lamp shade with brown tissue paper. Use a mixture of 2 parts white glue to 1 part water to adhere the paper to the shade. Paint on the glue, add tissue, and paint on more glue, until the whole shade is covered. Use the same technique to add animal-print tissue paper to the lamp base.

② Create three large paper pieced animals by increasing the size of the pattern found on p. 208 to a size that will fit nicely on the lamp shade. Detailed paper piecing instructions can be found in Chapter 6. Ink the edges of each completed animal and adhere it to the lamp shade with photo tape.

To complete the lamp, use hot glue to attach some trim around the bottom edge of the shade. The finished lamp is ready for display. Decoupage lamp shades to match seasons of the year to allow you to change the décor of any room in your house.

Scrapbooking on Canvas

Scrapbookers can create beautiful wall art simply by moving their craft out of the album and placing it on a canvas. The same techniques used in traditional scrapbooking convert well to making home art pieces.

① Paint a canvas with a color you choose. The canvas shown here has been painted with a crackle medium between coats.

② Once the paint is completely dry, you can add paper or adhesive-backed fabric to create a scrapbook page background.

③ Add photos and journaling words to the canvas using a tacky tape or liquid glue.

④ To complete the canvas, add appropriate embellishments such as ribbon, brads, buttons, or flowers.

The completed scrapbook art canvas is ready for display on the wall of your home or office. Art canvas projects also make excellent gifts.

Crafting Home Décor 191

Sparkle Lights

Add some sparkle to your special occasions with this easy paper craft project. Glittered die-cuts are added to a string of mini-lights to bring glitzy twinkle to nighttime events.

① Begin by die-cutting enough shapes to cover at least half of the lights on the string. Punch a hole in the center of each die-cut no larger than the diameter of the light bulb.

② Run the die-cuts through a Xyron adhesive machine to add a smooth and even layer of adhesive over the entire die-cut.

③ Cover each die-cut shape in extra-fine glitter. The finer the glitter, the better coverage your shape will have.

④ Add the glittered shapes to a string of mini-lights. The string shown here has been strung with flowers and leaves for outdoor wedding decorations.

This string shows that by switching out the flowers for red, white, and blue stars, the lights would make gorgeous Independence Day decorations.

Crafting Home Décor 193

Tween Mobile

A mobile is not just for hanging over a baby's crib. You can make a super-cool, summer-themed mobile perfect for hanging above a pre-teen's desk or adorning a window.

① To begin, gather supplies such as stickers, sticker letters, chipboard stickers, embroidered stickers, chipboard, and patterned paper. You also need fishing line, jump rings, a few hangers, wire cutters, and round nose pliers.

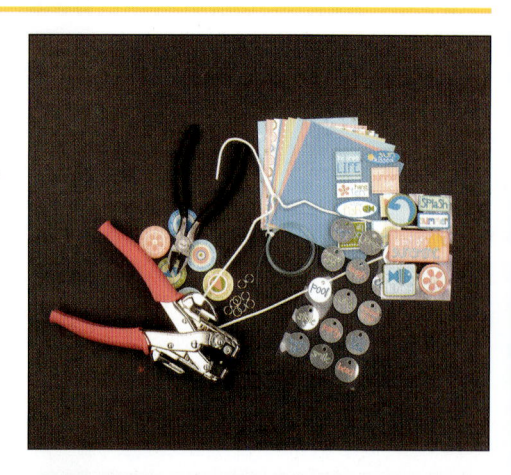

② Use heavy-duty wire cutters to snip off straight sections of wire hanger.

③ Use a pair of round nose or needle nose pliers to bend the end of the wire around into a circle.

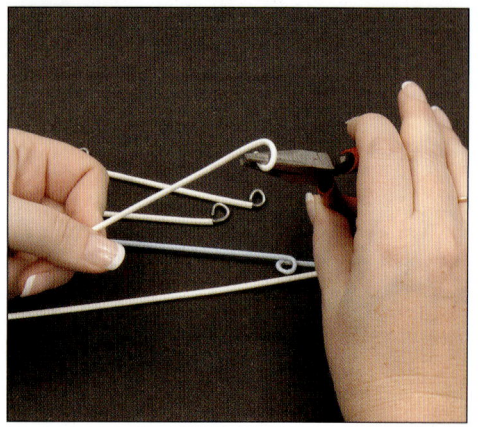

Paper Crafts VISUAL Quick Tips

④ Punch chipboard circles and cover them with patterned paper.

⑤ Punch holes in the top and bottom of the circles.

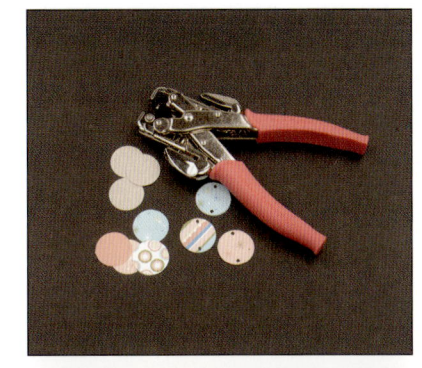

⑥ Create lines of pieces that will hang from the wires. Start by tying an 18" piece of fishing line through the top hole of a chipboard circle. Use jump rings to add additional items to the strand until you are happy with the length of the piece.

⑦ Add sticker letters or chipboard stickers to the fishing line by sandwiching the line between the pieces. Create enough strands to dangle off the end of each piece of wire. Adjust pieces as needed to balance the finished mobile.

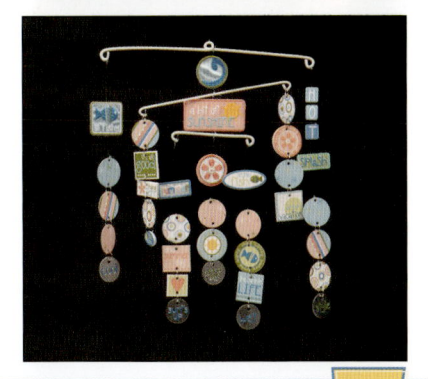

Crafting Home Décor   195

Art Clock

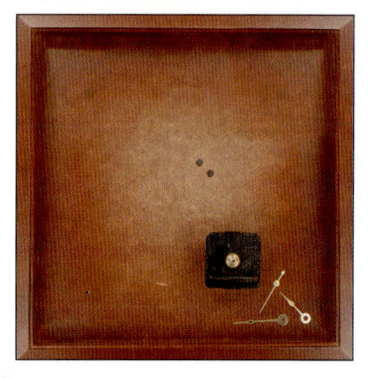

1. Create this beautiful clock to display your treasured family photos. To begin, you need the following: a clock kit; a shadow box or a deeply recessed picture frame; chipboard cut to the size of the frame; scrapbook supplies; and photos.

2. Arrange a scrapbook page layout, starting by covering the chipboard with background paper. Make sure to mark where the clock will be located on the layout.

3. Drill a hole in the center of where the clock will be located.

4. Insert the clock mechanism through the hole and add washers and hands to the front.

Paper Crafts VISUAL Quick Tips

The completed clock is an elegant keepsake to hang on a wall at work or home.

Crafting Home Décor

Letter Blocks

Letters make excellent home décor. You can embellish initials, full names, or inspirational words. These baby letters would make a great gift for new parents.

---

① To begin, select paper board or wooden letters that spell out the desired word. The letters shown here come in a kit from EK Success.

② Cover the letters with patterned paper and sand the edges.

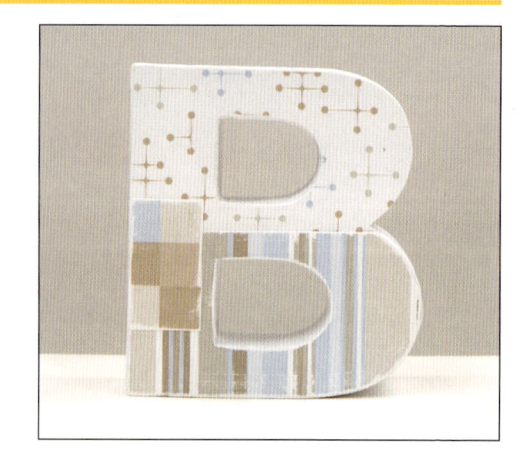

③ Complete each letter by adding embellishments such as ribbon, buttons, and silk flowers.

The completed letters can be hung on the wall or stacked on a dresser. To spell out a word vertically, you may want to hot glue letters to a long piece of ribbon before hanging them.

Crafting Home Décor

Appendix: Patterns

The popularity of paper crafting has caused an explosion in the number of companies that manufacture fantastic products. Tools, papers, stickers, embellishments, and even adhesives come in every shape, size, and color. Here you can find the patterns used for several of the projects in earlier chapters.

Note: *You'll find the names of the manufacturers whose products were used on the projects throughout this book at www.wiley.com/go/papercrafts*

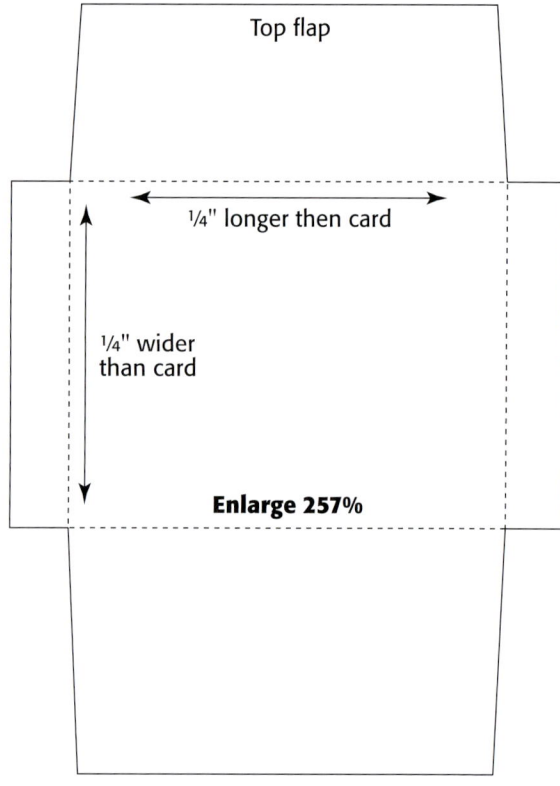

Top flap

←— ¼" longer then card —→

¼" wider than card

Enlarge 257%

Envelope (Chapter 3)

Enlarge 124%

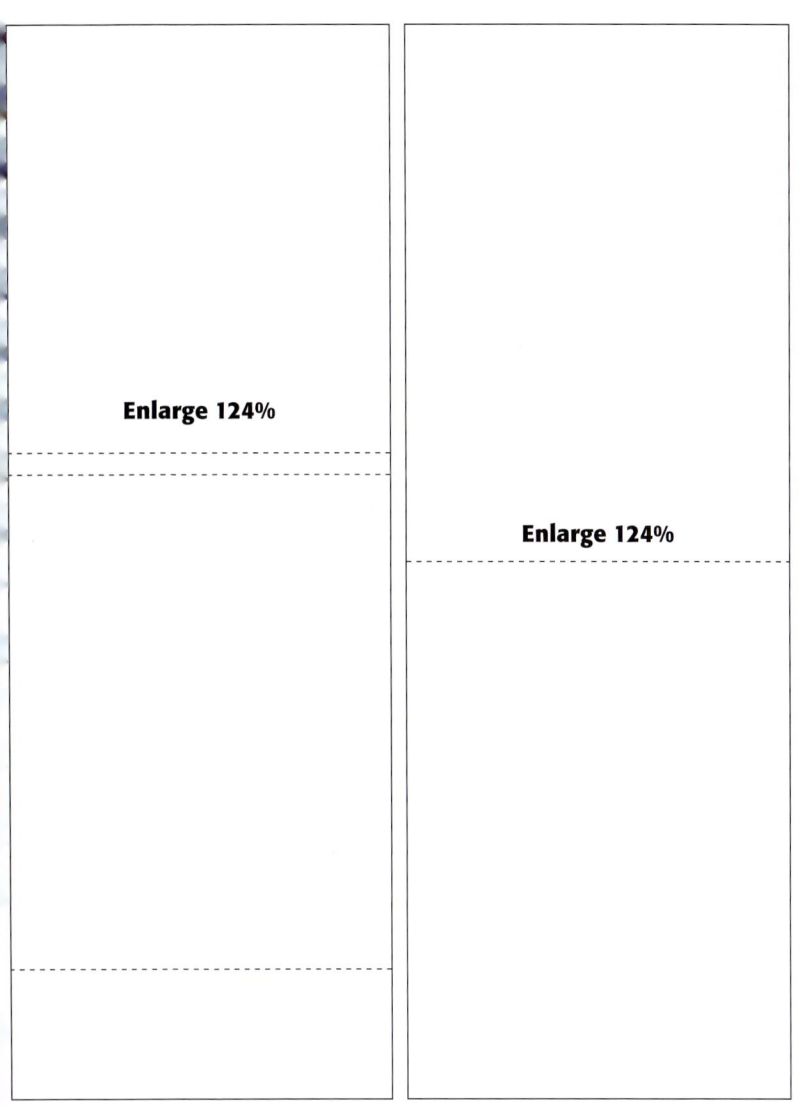

Enlarge 124%

*Matchbook Cover and Matchbook Inside
Pages (Chapter 3)*

Appendix: Patterns 201

Enlarge 124%

Matchbook Invitation Teapot (Chapter 3)

File Folder (Chapter 3)

Appendix: Patterns

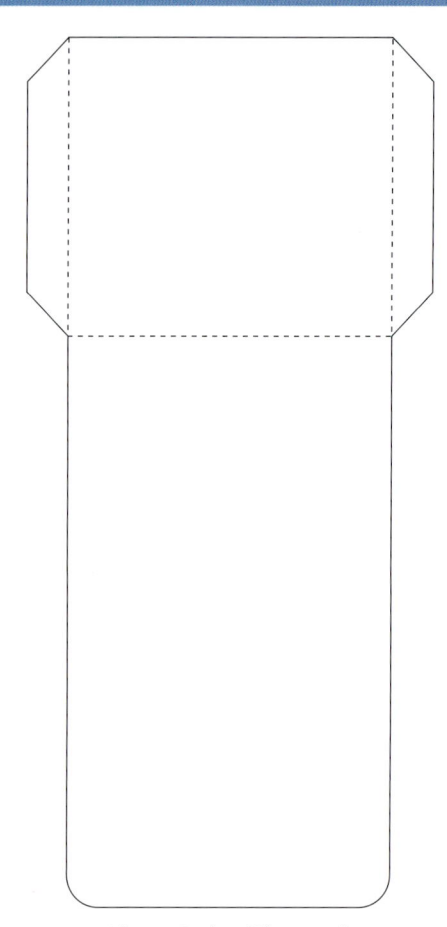

Library Pocket (Chapter 3)

——— Cut lines
- - - - - - fold lines

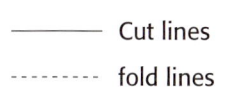

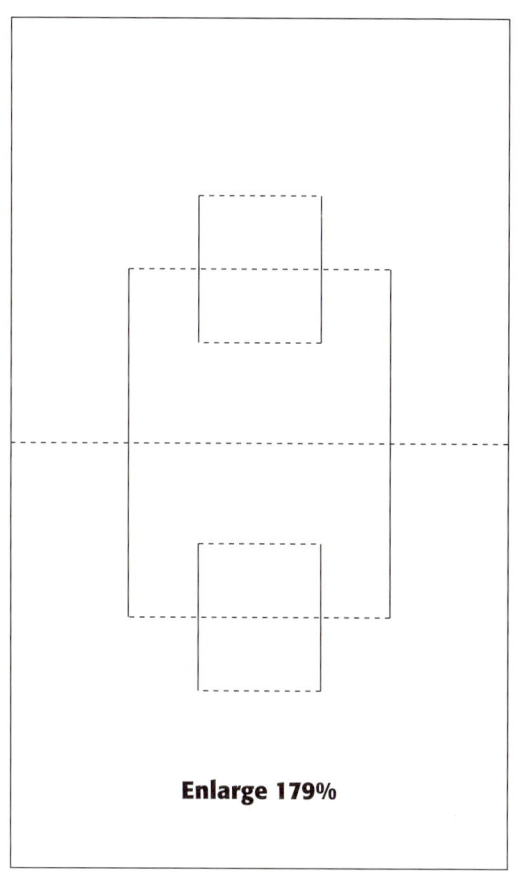

Enlarge 179%

Pop-Up Card Template (Chapter 3)

Appendix: Patterns

Enlarge 185%

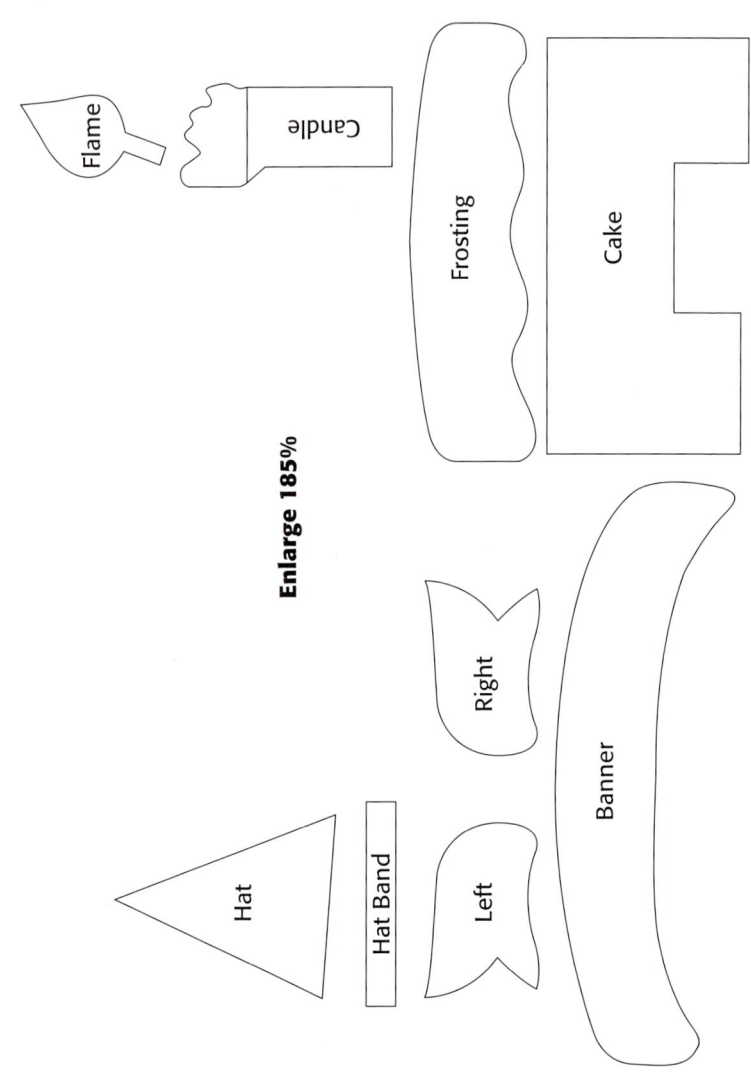

Pop-Up Card Birthday Pieces (Chapter 3)

206 **Paper Crafts VISUAL Quick Tips**

Enlarge 101%

Plate

Pop-Up Card Birthday Base (Chapter 3)

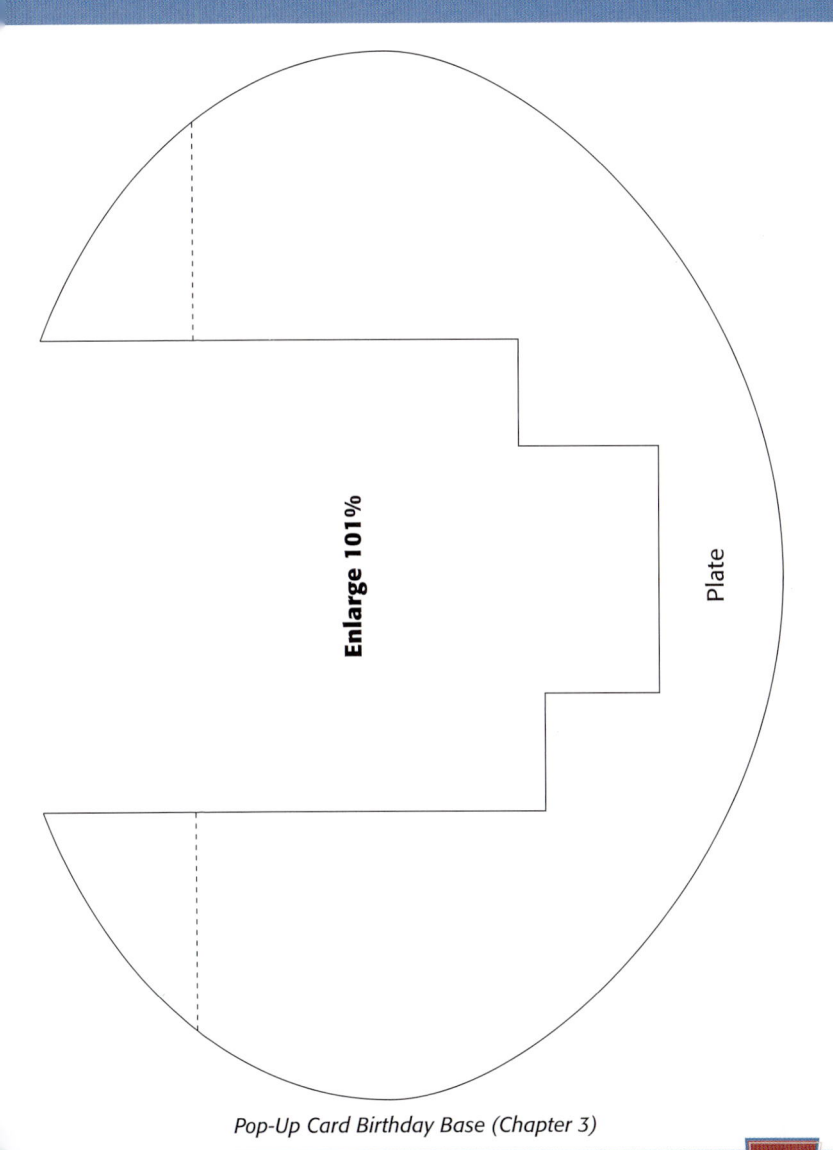

Appendix: Patterns

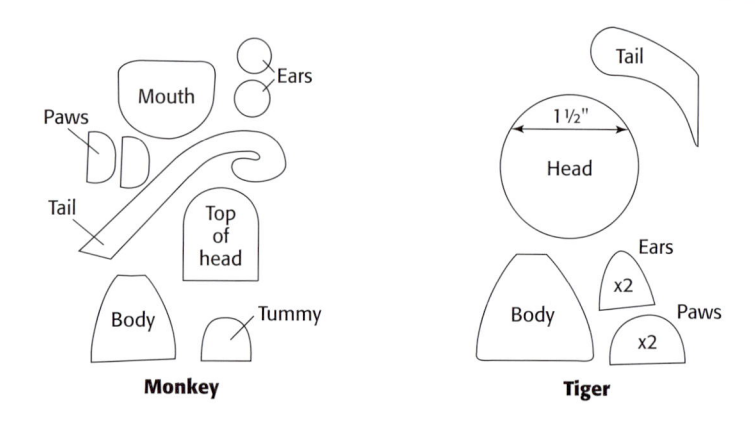

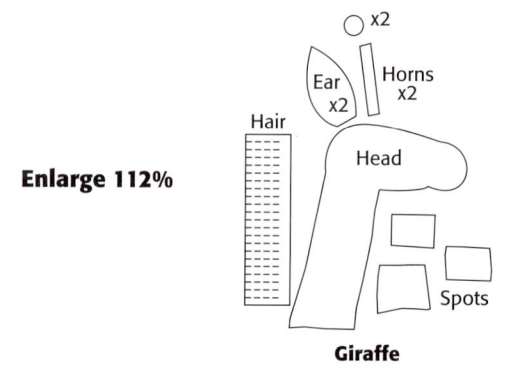

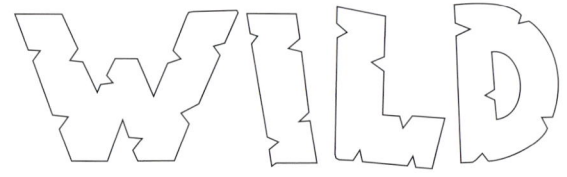

Monkey
- Ears
- Mouth
- Paws
- Tail
- Top of head
- Body
- Tummy

Tiger
- Tail
- Head (1½")
- Ears x2
- Body
- Paws x2

Enlarge 112%

Giraffe
- x2
- Ear x2
- Horns x2
- Hair
- Head
- Spots

Paper Piecing Pattern (Chapter 6)

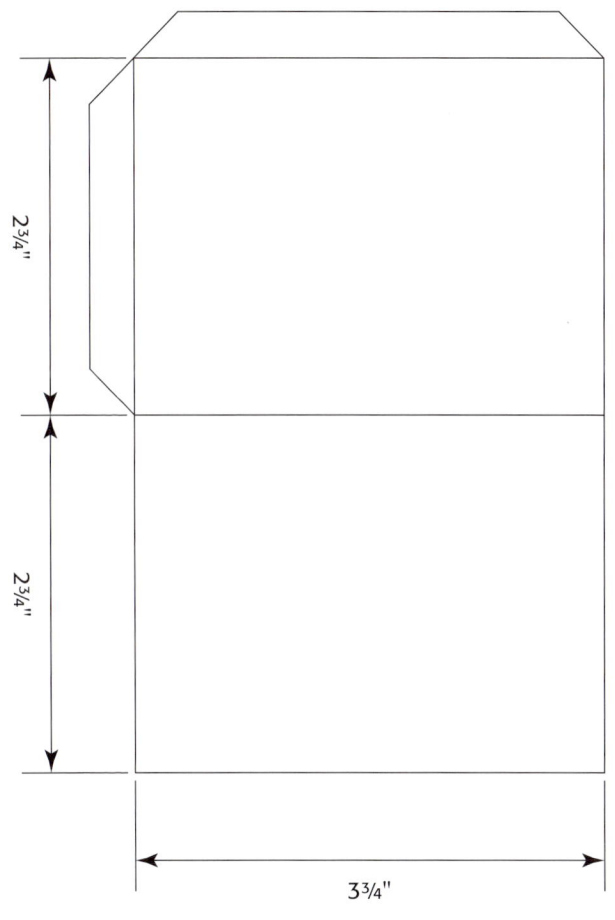

Vellum Pocket (Chapter 6)

Index

A
accordion book, 74–77
address labels, 37
adhesives, 6–7, 192
albums, 20–21
analogous color scheme, 12
anniversary cards, 99, 131, 161
anniversary-theme book, 78–80
art clock, 196–197
art journaling, 172–175

B
baby announcement cards, 43, 51
beads, 155–156
birthday cards, 54–59, 149, 161
bleach stamping, 94–95
bone folders, 35
book making
    accordion book, 74–77
    container books, 82–85
    envelope book, 70–72
    friends paper bag book, 81
    mini-books, 62–69
    overview, 62–63
    paper bag book, 78–80
    travel-themed envelope book, 73
borders, geometric, 112–113
brads, 134–135, 140, 142
brass stencils, 9, 52
bridal shower invitations, 44–45

C
canvas, 168–169, 190–191
card making
    birthday card organizer, 54–56
    card gallery, 58–61
    dry embossing cards and envelopes, 52–53
    envelope sizes, 34
    file folder cards, 42–43
    folding, 35
    library pocket card, 44–45
    making envelopes, 36–37
    match book invitations, 40–41
    overview, 32–33
    photo greeting cards, 38–39
    pop-up cards, 49–51
    recipe book, 57
    scoring, 35
    window cards, 46–48
chalk inks, 9, 91, 103
chalks, 9, 111
chipboard monogram letters, 160–161
Christmas cards, 100–101
clock, art, 196–197
collage wall art, 168–169
colors, 10–15
container books, 82–85
corner rounder punch, 36, 44, 84
crumpling paper, 109
cutting tools, 5

D
decorated photo frames, 186–187
decoupaged lamp, 188–189
diaries, art, 172
die-cuts, 146–147, 192
direct to paper inking, 110
double stamping, 98–99
dry embossing, 52–53
dye-based ink pads, 90

E
embossing, 90, 91, 100–102, 148
envelope book, 70–72
envelopes
    dry embossing, 52–53
    embossing, 53
    making, 36–37
    sizes, 34
    template, 36–37
    vellum, 124–125
eyelets, 80, 132–133, 140, 142

F

fabric, printing on, 144–145
family history, 19
felt, 185
file folder cards, 42–43
flowers, 129–131, 136–137
flower stamp, 96–97
foam adhesive, 6
foam letters, 154–157
foam squares, 6
foam stamps, 89
folded paper ribbon, 122–123
folding paper, 35
fonts, letter, 92, 149
formal cards, 100–101
frames, 24, 186–187

G

genealogies, 19
geometric borders, 112–113
get well cards, 131
giraffe pattern, 116–118, 188
glitter, 102–103, 193
glue, 7, 91, 127, 170–171, 188
greeting cards. See card making
grommets, 132

H

heat embossing, 100–101
heat guns, 100–101
heavyweight paper, 4
hole punches, 132

I

images, art journal, 172, 175
image stamps, 89
inking, 73, 110
Inkjet printer transparencies, 142
ink pads, 90–91
invitations, 44–45, 48, 119, 161
ironing paper, 108–109

J

journaling, 22, 39, 43, 111, 172–175

L

labels, 37, 148–149
lamps, paper pieced, 188–189
layered letters, 152–153
layout, scrapbook page, 22
leaves, quilling, 129
letter blocks, 198–199
lettering, stamp, 92–93
lettering styles
    chipboard monogram letters, 160–161
    clay letters, 162–163
    label maker lettering, 148–149
    layered letters, 152–153
    overview, 138–139
    printing, 140–147
    shaker letters, 154–155
    stamping, 150–151
    stencil paste letters, 164–165
    tag shaker titles, 156–157
    templates, 150–151
lettering tools, 8
library pocket card, 44–45
life events, recording, 19
light boxes, 52
lightweight paper, 4
lights, sparkle, 192–193

M

magnetic stamps, 88
markers, 103
match book invitations, 40–41
matting techniques, 25
metallic rub-ons, 9
mini-books, 62–69
mobiles, tween, 194–195
monochromatic colors, 11–12
mouse pads, 134–135
multiple photographs, matting, 25

N

numbers, chipboard, 161

O

organizers, birthday card, 54–56

Index

P

paints, 9, 85, 182
paper
    crumpling, 109
    folded ribbon, 122–123
    inking, 110
    ironing, 109
    online piecing patterns, 119
    patterned, 4
    piecing, 51, 116–119
    sanding, 109
    sewing, 120–121
    tearing, 108
    types of, 4
paper bag book, 78–80
paper clay, 162
paper pieced lamp, 188–189
paper punches, 112–113
paper trimmers, 5
patterned paper, 4
patterns
    creating, 119
    file folder, 42
    giraffe, 116–118, 188
    match book, 40
    online, 119
    pop-up card, 49
    vellum envelope, 122–123
pens, 8
photographs
    cube puzzles, 184–185
    focal point, 22, 26
    frames, 186–187
    matting, 24–25
    preserving, 18
    supporting, 22
    on wooden cubes, 182–183
photo greeting cards, 38–39
photo tape, 6, 65–66
phrase stamps, 89
pieced stamping, 96–97
piecing, paper, 116–119
pigment inks, 90, 100
plastic templates, 9
pocket envelopes, 124–125
polymer clay, 162
pool party invitation, 48
pop-up cards, 49–51
post-bound albums, 20
printers, 144–145
printing
    on cork, 144–145
    on die-cuts, 146–147
    on fabric, 144–145
    on ribbon, 144–145
    on tags, 146–147
    on transparencies, 142–143
    on vellum, 140–141
punches, 5, 112–113
pushpins, 134–135
puzzles, photo cube, 184–185

Q

quilling, 126–131

R

recipe book, 57
ribbon
    accordion books, 76–77
    mini-books, 66
    paper bag books, 80
    printing on, 144–145
roses, quilling, 130–131
rubber stamps, 88, 145
rub on ink, 110
rub-ons, metallic, 9

S

sanding, paper, 109
scissors, 5
scrapbooks
    albums, 20
    album sizes, 21
    on canvas, 190–191
    chipboard letters, 160
    creating focal points, 26–27
    envelopes, 70
    first pages, 23
    gallery, 28–31
    importance, 18–19
    journaling folders, 43
    layout, 22, 26–27, 113, 115

library card pockets, 45
match books, 41
matting techniques, 25
mini-books, 64
overview, 16–17
paper ribbon, 122–123
printed, 141–147
silk flower squares, 137
torn paper background, 108
vellum envelopes, 124–125
serendipity squares, 114–115
series, artist trading card, 177
sewing books, 79
sewing paper, 120–121
shaker letters, 154–155
shape cutters, 5
silk flowers, 136–137
Sizzix die cases, 82–83
slotted quilling tools, 126
sparkle lights, 192–193
specialty paper, 4
spiral bound albums, 20
spray painting, 85
square punches, 46–47
stamping
    with bleach, 94–95
    double, 98–99
    embellishing, 102–105
    heat embossing, 100–101
    ink pads and cleaners, 90–91
    lettering, 92–93, 150–151
    overview, 8, 86–87
    pieced, 96–97
    serendipity squares, 114
    stamp cleaners, 90–91
    types of stamps, 88–89

stamp pads, 8
stencil paste letters, 164–165
stencils, 9, 52, 111, 164–165
stickers, 51, 194–195
stitches, sewing, 120
strap-hinge albums, 20
stripes, 23

T

tacky tape, 6
tags, 81, 146–147
tag shaker titles, 156–157
tape runners, 6
templates, 9, 36–37, 150–151
text, art journal, 173
texture, paper, 109
Thanksgiving card, 48
thank you cards, 43, 60–61
three-dimensional letters, 162
three-ring binding albums, 20
tissue paper decoupage, 170–171
trading cards, artist, 176–179
transparencies, printing on, 142–143
travel-themed envelope book, 73
triadic colors, 11, 13
tween mobile, 194–195

V

vellum, 124–125, 140–141

W

wall art, collage, 168–169
watermark pads, 91
window cards, 46–48
wire, 194
wooden photo cubes, 182–183
word stamps, 89

Index 213

Perfectly portable!

With handy, compact *VISUAL*™ *Quick Tips* books, you're in the know wherever you go.

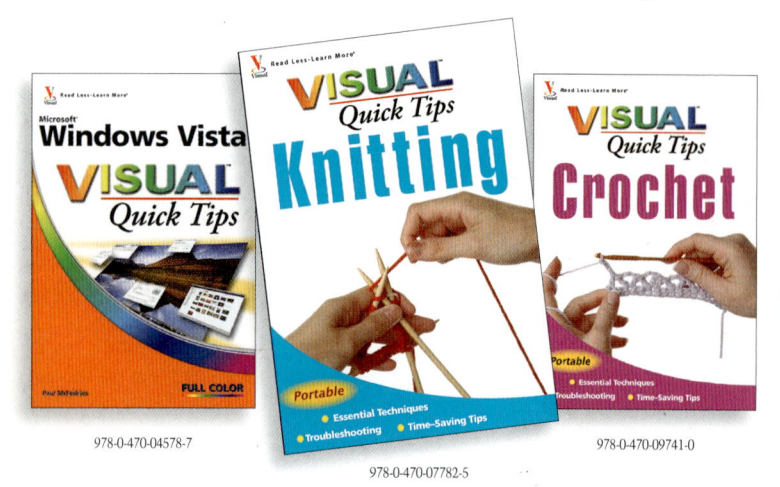

978-0-470-04578-7

978-0-470-07782-5

978-0-470-09741-0

All *VISUAL*™ *Quick Tips* books pack a lot of info into a compact 5 x 7 $^1/_8$" guide you can toss into your tote bag or brief case for ready reference.

Look for these and other *VISUAL*™ *Quick Tips* books wherever books are sold.

Read Less-Learn More®

Visual
An Imprint of WILEY

Wiley, the Wiley logo, the VISUAL logo, Read Less-Learn More, Teach Yourself VISUALLY, and VISUAL Quick Tips are trademarks or registered trademarks of John Wiley & Sons, Inc. and/or its affiliates. All other trademarks are the property of their respective owners.